LONDON TRANSPORT

BUSES & COACHES

1952

LONDON TRANSPORT

BUSES & COACHES

1952

John A.S. Hambley

Published in 1993 by
IMAGES

in conjunction with
JOHN A. S. HAMBLEY
7 Linden Road,
Dunstable,
Beds. LU5 4NZ

British Library Cataloguing in Publication Data
A catalogue record for this book is available from the British Library

ISBN 1 897817 10 X

Front cover photograph:
This picture is as one likes to remember TF9, standing in the sunshine at a typical tourist venue on the "Seeing London Tour" with a lovely Riley saloon of pre-war vintage to keep it company.

Back cover photograph:
Three tram replacement bus routes can be seen in this picture taken at New Cross Gate. On the left a bus on route 172 heads for Forest Hill Station, formerly tram service 35. In the middle is STL854 on route 182, formerly tram service 46 and on the right RTL908 is on route 36A, formerly tram service 66 although that ran between Forest Hill and Victoria rather than the Brockley Rise to West Kilburn run of its successor. The date is 14th July and already the trams are a nine day old memory. (A.B. Cross)

Designed and produced by Images (Publishing) Malvern Ltd.
Printed and bound in Great Britain by Severnside Printers Limited, Upton-upon-Severn, Worcs.

Chelsham garage was home to C59 for a good number of years and here on the 17th August it lays over in a sylvan setting while working a "swinger" to Oxted, Barrow Green Road. By 1956 the bus was operating for a contractor on Hayling Island where its size doubtless matched the tank engines then providing the railway service to that part of the world. (J.H. Aston)

Acknowledgements

As usual, the source of the illustrations in this book are individually acknowledged but I would like to thank the many people who have made their use possible, either by providing negatives or prints, or by lending items from their private collections for reproduction. These include James H. Aston, J.F. Bearman, Ronald G. Bristow, C. Carter, Alan B. Cross, John Gascoine, J.C. Gillham, B.J. Harding, W.J. Haynes, Roy Hobbs, D.W.K. Jones, Kevin Lane, S.E. Letts, Sheila Taylor of the London Transport Museum, The London Trolleybus Preservation Society, Ian Maclean, Roy Marshall, Geoff Morant, Omnibus Society, J.H. Price, David A. Ruddom, P.F. Sapte, Sabena Belgian World Airlines, John Smith of Lens of Sutton, John G.S. Smith, R.H. Simpson, and Anthony M. Wright.

Again, I would extend sincere thanks to the PSV circle for continued use of information from their publications and in particular to John G.S. Smith and David Ruddom for their assistance. To John for his enthusiasm and help with this project and to David for the considerable assistance and advice provided in writing the hopefully informative captions and text and then committing the results to the word processor. Finally, on a personal note, to my wife Iris and David Ruddom's wife Enid for their support and understanding.

Publisher's Note

There are a few illustrations which have no indication as to their origin. This is because the prints used bear no information and research has not provided any clues to this. If this can be rectified in later volumes I shall be pleased to do so on receipt of the information and offer apologies to anyone to whom appreciation may therefore be lacking. From the many letters received it is obvious that this series of books forms a link between enthusiasts and historians with the various custodians and owners of the photographs used. It is most encouraging to add further photographers to the series whose work appears in this volume or will be seen in later books. Please let me know if you have any black and white prints or negatives which could possibly be used in the years still to be covered.

Introduction

Since this is the fifth book in this series looking at the buses and coaches once operated by London Transport and, indeed, 1952 was something of a watershed in the post-war development of London Transport, it seems appropriate to briefly re-cap on how the fleet and routes had developed since the ending of World War II.

The fleet, in line with those of many other operators, had suffered considerably from the ravages of war during the six years of hostilities. Several garages and many vehicles had been damaged or destroyed by the Luftwaffe. New replacement vehicles were strictly rationed and deliveries to London Transport had not matched the required replacement programme. Coupled to this, one must take into account the shortage of materials of the immediate post war years.

Once the tide had changed following D-day and the liberation of Europe had begun, deliveries of new vehicles became a reality albeit very slowly at first but gradually gathering momentum until the London fleet of buses and coaches began to resemble something of its pre-war quality. A number of ways of getting the fleet back up to standard were put into force. Firstly there were the interim orders placed for a number of smaller batches of buses which were quickly put into service and these comprised the last deliveries of the B, D and G classes, deliveries of which had commenced during the war. Further STD, T and STL vehicles were added to the existing numbers already in service and a new generation of TD class vehicles, this time single-deckers, were obtained. Orders for the post war RT family of buses were placed and the initial trickle, which subsequently built to a flood of these new vehicles being put on the road over the next seven years, was started.

Certain older vehicles of some classes were sent to outside contractors for refurbishment and rebuilding. Finally the worn out fleet was systematically disposed of using various formulae for their withdrawal from service with the peak year being 1949, when no fewer than 1,638 buses and coaches were lost from the streets of London forever. Mention must also be made of the trams which were finally replaced by diesel buses, rather than by trolleybuses, which had been the intention before the War.

So much had happened in this short period in the history of London Transport that by the end of 1952 the ST, G, LTC and double-deck LT classes together with all the trams had been totally withdrawn from service. The remaining non-RT family double deckers comprised the STL class, which by now was reduced to a little over 600 vehicles from its one time total of 2,701; the pre-war and post-war STD class vehicles; a few Bs; the highbridge Ds and the solitary post-war Guy, G436. On the single deck front, alongside the growing number of new RF vehicles, the C, T, Q, TF and TD classes were still represented together with the residue of the single deck LTs and a few CRs.

The number of new buses and coaches delivered to London Transport was impressive, with no fewer than 3,851 RTs having been delivered since the war together with 1,406 of the RTL class. All of the 500 strong RTW class plus 160 SRTs, 76 RLHs, 15 RFWs and the single Guy Arab G436 had now been delivered. 387 of the latest single deck class, the underfloor engined RF type, were also now on the streets of the capital and mention should be made of the rebuilt RTC1 and STL2477 which appeared during this period and were still in service.

On the route scene developments had been slow, governed by the vehicle situation and then the need to replace the trams. There were some new routes and extensions, most of which have been covered in previous volumes of this series.

In 1952 however, for the first time since the War it was possible to envisage some expansionist development of services. In the embryonic New

Towns of Crawley, Harlow, Hemel Hempstead and Stevenage new services appeared for the first time to supplement the long standing trunk routes which passed through the areas. Increased frequencies and small extensions were made in the large post-war housing estates at New Addington, Harold Hill, Aveley and Sheerwater. Several new links were forged both in the Central and Country Areas but it must not be forgotten that while these new services were being developed passenger miles were already declining and reductions in frequencies, particularly on Sundays and in the evenings were becoming a regular feature as new schedules were prepared. In fact, between the beginning and ending of 1952 around 200 fewer vehicles were needed for the Sunday schedules.

Bus routes replacing tram services were, broadly speaking, unadventurous and although a few useful extensions and links were introduced, in the main the well worn furrows of the tram tracks were followed and it was not until the following years that the old pattern of tram services began to dissolve and lose the evidence of its origins. For example, in August 1952 there were no fewer than 13 daytime bus routes running along the Victoria Embankment, which was always inconveniently situated for the obvious traffic objectives of the Strand and Fleet Street. Nowadays, of course, none remain.

A number of memorable events took place during 1952. The final three stages of tram conversion took place eliminating in April the thrill of a ride down the Kingsway Subway. The third of these conversions, as mentioned above, marked the end of tram operation in London in the early hours of the morning of Sunday 6th July. As originally planned, this final conversion would have been a much smaller affair and would have taken place in October but with the involvement of a small number of pre-war STLs and 2RT2s it was realised that the trams could all go in the July conversion programme and so the die was cast for London's "Last Tram Day" and the citizens said farewell to their faithful steeds in grand style.

The former Eastern National routes which had been operated since the previous October in the Grays area were fully integrated into the London Transport system on the 2nd January and the Argent Street garage at Grays ceased to be operational.

Three specially prepared buses, in the shape of RT2775, RT2776 and RTL1307, made a historic trip to the North American continent starting on March 8th and ending in August when all three vehicles together with the support transport were lined up on Horse Guards Parade on the 20th for a welcome home ceremony. The RTL was the only one at the time to carry a Weymann built body.

The nation was saddened in February by the death of King George VI and with the coronation of Queen Elizabeth II due to take place in the following year, many STL class buses were being overhauled in the latter part of 1952 and stored at a number of locations in readiness for the extra work load this event would bring to the capital.

Detailed figures of the fleet movement for the year were as follows. New vehicles delivered were 422 RTs (204 with Park Royal and 218 with Weymann bodywork); 151 RTLs (150 with Park Royal and the solitary RTL1307 with Weymann bodywork); 276 RFs (99 being new Central Area buses and the remainder Green Line coaches, all with Metro-Cammell bodywork); 56 RLHs (24 for the Central Area and the remainder in Country Area green, all with Weymann lowbridge bodywork). This made a total of 905 new vehicles delivered. Although not covered by the terms of reference of this book it should perhaps be mentioned that the final 50 new Q1 class trolleybuses were also delivered in 1952.

On the withdrawal side, 592 vehicles were withdrawn from passenger service 224 STLs, 151 Gs, 68 single deck LTs, 48 Ts, 13 TFs, 10 Bs, 16 Qs, 1 CR, 49 Ds, the last 6 STs, and the last 6 LTCs. By the end of the year therefore all the utility Guys, almost half of the Bristols and the first of the Daimlers had been withdrawn and with the elimination of the trams, LT was rapidly getting back to a fleet of pre-war standards and modern appearance.

Surely the back platform isn't coming loose on a one year old vehicle - or has the conductor dropped a tanner? (2½p to younger readers!). The scene is Kew Green and Weymann bodied RT4214 works the Sunday 83A route from Alperton garage. (J.H. Aston)

This rear view is of LT1114 working on route 227 from Bromley garage on the 13th May. This was the vehicle rebuilt by Sunny Doors Ltd. of Southend in the winter of 1944/45 and while it did not have any of the distinctive appearance of the rebuilt LT1131, which was done by Twiddy of Norwich, afficionados of the "scooter" will observe something odd about the rear profile when compared to the original version. (A.B. Cross)

STL1919 together with a cyclist who appears to be giving a friend a lift are the sole users of Dartford High Street. Overhead wiring for the trolleybus service 696 turns into Market Street and the shops in the background are a far cry from the High Street frontages of today. (L.T.P.S.)

Eccleston Bridge on the 22nd June sees T636 laying over having worked in from Windsor on Green Line route 718 as relief duty WR110. (J.C. Gillham)

Taken in the vicinity of Wembley Stadium on the same day, 3rd May, as the photograph of former ST922 at Alperton, which appears elsewhere in this book, the chassis of 811J was that of former STL377, which was withdrawn from service at Turnham Green garage in August 1948. The body was scrapped a year later but the chassis re-emerged with this body by Kenex in December 1949 as a 7 ton towing lorry, lasting in this form until June 1964. (A.B. Cross)

STD125 only a few months before receiving its 1953 overhaul which would deprive it of its early post war livery and bring it into line with more of the fleet which was becoming increasingly standardised on the single between decks cream band relief. The bus is seen working the 167 route to Ilford Station from Debden where this damp view on the stand in Willingale Road is taken. (C. Carter)

Bromley garage would be the last operational home for LT1143 before its eventual disposal to Cohens, the dealers of London, in early 1953. Route 227 would then become RF operated and these six wheeled vehicles would be but a memory at the Gordon Arms terminus in Chislehurst. (John Gascoine collection)

Q21 was repainted into Central Area livery during 1950, having up to that point always been a Country Area green vehicle. Now enjoying a further lease of life, it was among the last to be withdrawn from service during 1953. Of interest is the minimum fare board, carried to the rear of the front entrance door. This feature was intended to dissuade passengers using this particular route from making short journeys from the centre of Kingston where other facilities existed. Thus it was ensured that space would be available for those travelling to outlying destinations. It is the 26th April and the bus is seen at the cross roads in Esher High Street with a branch of the then still independent Westminster Bank in the background.
(J.C. Gillham)

Although recorded as being disposed of to R. Daniels of Rainham for scrap in January 1950, very much alive ex-STL2090 is seen here being used as a showman's vehicle. A very professional conversion has taken place at sometime to the bus. Half the upper deck depth has been removed and the roof, which formerly carried a route number box, has been replaced on the remaining half level deck. It appears that the exhaust pipe has been extended to discharge at the new roof level.

As with other photographs which have appeared in this series of books, the changes which have taken place in Kingston over the years sometimes makes comparisons with the present day scene difficult. Q53 followed by T17 drives out of Clarence Street which is now one-way in the opposite direction. Behind the vehicles on the left is the old Kingston Empire built, as prominently shown, in 1910, while on the right is the Granada, home of a famous cinema organ. (D.W.K. Jones)

LT1187 is seen here in Carshalton Road, Sutton, long before the cinema alongside was demolished to make way for redevelopment and later road improvements. The unmistakable lines of its Marshalls of Cambridge rebuilt body hide the fact that the bus is now over twenty years old. (A.M. Wright)

The date is 10th May, the location Crystal Palace and the vehicle "Tunnel" STL1867. This bus appears in the 1949 book but since then it has been through Chiswick Works for an overhaul and now wears the latest livery style. It was sold to W.A., E. & V. Jolly of Norton for further service from around the middle of 1954. (J.H. Aston)

T662 carries Green Line name and colour scheme while operating one of the special journeys on the 424 route between Horley and Outwood worked by Crawley garage. Although a float of three spare bodies was built in 1938/9 when these coaches were being put into service, no exchanges had taken place within the 266 strong class until war damaged vehicles made use of the extra bodies in 1944. Thereafter the number of body exchanges could be counted on the fingers of two hands but T662 happens to be one of them, exchanging its body in March 1946 for that originally carried by T652. The shop immediately behind the T has quite a number of enamel plates, highly sought after by collectors nowadays, advertising Spratt's animal products. (A.B. Cross)

Although later in the year Amersham garage received some additional lowbridge RLHs which interworked on to route 359, in April they received an additional RT which allowed the route to be worked by that class of bus. This was the route which for many years was worked jointly with the Eastern National Omnibus Company. Here one of Amersham's earlier RTs, 3889, stands at Kingsbury Square, Aylesbury before returning to Amersham down through Wendover and the upper part of the Misbourne Valley. (R.H.G. Simpson)

The Square, Dunstable provides the resting place for Tring's T616 on the 1st June. This neat and orderly transport scene presents a very different aspect to the present day varied liveries and origins of companies now serving this Bedfordshire town. The bus here is working the rarely seen 352 route which only operated a few journeys on four days a week through the delightful countryside around Dagnall and Ashridge to Berkhamsted in Hertfordshire. (A.B. Cross)

Now here is a real caravan in the shape of single deck LT1200! Having lost its wheels the registration plate would seem to be superfluous. Nevertheless it is obviously someone's pride and joy with added door to the saloon and windows fitted with curtains. No documentation details of the whereabouts of the camp site or for how long the caravan was in use are known but all the same a fine end to a vehicle which had served Londoners for over 18 years. What a pity the preservation movement had not got going in 1952. (L.T.P.S.)

The 22nd June does not appear to have been a very nice summer's day as Hackney's RTW323 journeys through the dismal surroundings of north-east London. The following month Hackney was to receive a new allocation of RTLs for this route but previously they had used spare RTWs on the Sunday allocation as seen here. I have not been able to discover the significance of the neat little circle in the middle of the cream band at the front of the vehicle but it appears on other photographs of Hackney RTWs of the period as well. (A.B. Cross)

RTL1161 equipped for full blinds but here making poor use of the available space. Since route 120A from the Civil Engineer at Greenford to Hounslow Heath was worked by Southall garage and this is a Wandsworth allocated vehicle, it was obviously on a short term loan at the time this picture was taken.

LTC12 had been withdrawn from service in October 1951 but on the 27th May it sits patiently outside the ticket stores in Chiswick, no doubt contemplating its fate. Not very much is known of this class of vehicle after their disposal to a number of dealers in the 1953/4 period, save that at least a couple of the chassis were exported to Spain. (J.C. Gillham)

Pictured here at the bus station in Sarajevo, Yugoslavia, "No. 91" is unmistakably G36, courtesy of the staff at Upton Park garage who painted the fleet number on the rear dome. The bus is now operated by Autoprevoz of Sarajevo and carries registration number 6X0238. Being comparatively modern and much sought after, many ex-London Transport vehicles were now finding new operators in war torn Europe, which was still trying to recover from the aftermath of six years of hostilities. The ravages of Yugoslavian operation are already evident in the vehicle's condition. (J.C. Gillham)

Ealing Broadway, with B21 on its way to Ruislip High Street to which point route 97 had been extended from Greenford on 16th April in place of the single deck route 211. In the following year a number of these Bristols would be disposed of to the Lincolnshire Road Car Company for further service and included in this deal was B21. (C. Carter)

Whipsnade Zoo car park on Sunday 1st June and RTL603 has brought a day excursion from the Plumstead area to enjoy the animals and the Bedfordshire countryside. This is how one likes to remember this tourist attraction with, alongside the RTL, Green Line RTs from Romford (London Road) garage on the 726 limited stop service to Baker Street Station. (A.B. Cross)

New route 66A appeared in the Romford area for the first time with the introduction of the winter programme. A variant of the 66 it ran daily from Dagnam Park Drive in Harold Hill to the Parkside Hotel in Romford with a Mon-Fri peak extension to Newbury Park. One journey even went on to Leytonstone in the mornings. Worked by Forest Gate and Barking garages with SRTs it introduced an allocation of these vehicles to the latter shed for the first time. This is SRT150, one of Forest Gate's examples, coping with a hefty queue in Romford. (Geoff Morant)

Now 722J, this interesting vehicle photographed within Chiswick Works, was once STL193. The conversion to a 5½ ton tower wagon was completed by February 1948 some four months after the bus was withdrawn from service. While the body obviously owes its ancestry to the STL the actual tower came from another earlier lorry numbered 21H in the service vehicle fleet. (J.C. Gillham)

Part of St. Pancras Station, designed by Sir George Gilbert Scott, forms the background to Duple bodied D135. Scott's gothic design was originally submitted for the new Foreign Office but, following its rejection for this purpose, the Midland Railway benefitted by developing it as a very distinctive London terminal. While that building still stands the bus is no more, last heard of as being exported to Yugoslavia. (Roy Marshall)

The 329 route traversed some fairly minor country roads and even when it had reached its objective of Knebworth it ventured a little further west through the lanes to reach Nup End. Here, former coach TF27 samples the rural life at Hertford on the 10th May having been transferred in from Dorking only a couple of months earlier. (A.B. Cross)

On 13th July the PSV circle organised a visit to the City of Oxford Motor Services and the vehicle used was Enfield's STD26. Here it stands in Cowley Road garage, Oxford surrounded by the Guy Arabs and AEC Regents of the host company. (J.F. Bearman)

Its heyday as a Green Line coach over, T648 now plies the Kent countryside as an ordinary bus, although still showing many of its ancestral beginnings. This particular T, as with so many of the class, was exported after being withdrawn from service in January 1954. Notice the typical diminutive country area bus stop. (Lens of Sutton)

The administration block fronts the newly opened Garston garage with Mann Egerton bodied T798 standing alongside. The building behind houses the maintenance and parking area for the vehicles transferred to GR. The opening of the new garage on 18th June enabled the closure of the Leavesden Road garage and a re-arrangement of allocations on routes in the Watford area. (P.F. Sapte)

First put into service in September 1937, STL2175 was originally a 4/9STL15 finishing its days with London Transport as a 19STL16/2 as in the picture. The bus gained green livery when its original red Park Royal body was replaced by the one seen here upon the chassis of that vehicle being earmarked to become an SRT. The bus pauses opposite St. Albans garage on its journey on route 369 from Sandridge to Dunstable. (L.T.P.S.)

SRT111, spent its entire four and a half years of London service from the one garage, Chalk Farm and must have clocked up many miles on the 24 route between the long lived terminals of Hampstead Heath and Pimlico. STL2550 provided the chassis for this particular bus seen here in Camden Town.

(John Gascoine)

RT4163 is seen while operating the ex-Eastern National route 31, which ran between Grays and Tilbury via Dock Road. The bus is a standard 3RT8 with Weymann body. It was first put into service from Reigate garage in May 1951 and then moved on to Grays in December of that year, together with a small number of other RTs, in readiness for the complete integration of the former ENOC routes on 2nd January. An Opel Olympia 1.3 litre saloon together with a Morris Oxford follow the RT.

STL2562 appeared in the 1949 book on page 82 but it has received an overhaul in the intervening period although still retaining its STL16 body, number 132. It is seen here on route 371A, one of the cross-Grays routes introduced on 2nd January, this one running from Feenan Highway at Tilbury to Purfleet Station. It stands awaiting a fresh crew from the nearby Grays garage. (B.J. Harding)

LT1193 of Sutton garage is waiting to take up duties on route 213 to Kingston at Belmont Station. The crew take their ease on the longitudinal seats at the rear of the saloon on what is probably a cold 21st December, judging by the partly shielded radiator. The slip board warning of the minimum fare of 3d payable on journeys between Kingston Bus Station and Coombe Hill Road is prominently displayed. (A.B. Cross)

On the 14th July outside Peckham garage various RTs and an STL await their various duties including, in the forefront, RT1432. Still carrying the colour scheme in which it was delivered, the bus works from Nunhead garage on the circular 173 route. It is only just over a year before the bus would be overhauled and lose the cream relief to the upper deck windows. (A.B. Cross)

Duple bodied D162, with a Brush bodied example behind, is seen standing at Crystal Palace while waiting to take up duties on route 49 to Shepherds Bush on the 10th May. The picture quite clearly shows the comparison between the 1952 style livery of all over red with a cream band and the early post-war red and white scheme. (J.H. Aston)

Standing at the junction with the by-pass in East Ham Manor Way on the 22nd March, NCME bodied G311 shows off well its protruding radiator and what was arguably the most handsome looking of all the London utility vehicles. It is operating a short journey on the frequent 101 route to Royal Albert Dock. As with so many of this class, G311 was later used in Scotland, in this case by W. Alexander and Sons of Falkirk. (J.C. Gillham)

Weymann bodied T746, operating from the new Norbiton garage, waits at Hampton Court Station before commencing another journey on route 206 to Claygate. This batch of 50 post-war AEC Regals were powered by the 7.7 litre engine with crash gearboxes and triple-servo brakes and were much inferior to the specification of the later 1948 delivered batch. The bodies seated 35 when new but this was reduced by two when the transverse seat on each rear wheel arch was replaced by a single inward facing one. Twenty six of them lost a further seat when in the middle of 1954 the front offside double seat was replaced by a single one to give the conductor more standing space. (R.G. Bristow)

The last Daimler D type to be overhauled was Park Royal bodied D230. Seen here on the 18th November outside the body finishing shop at Chiswick Works it is awaiting final attention before moving back to Sutton garage. It spent a further twelve months in service with the Executive before being operated by the executors of Samuel Ledgard of Leeds. (J.D. Gillham)

Many readers will have seen this bus - indeed quite a few will have ridden on it - for this is ST922 which was miraculously rescued from the scrapyard by Prince Marshall and ran for several years on the Vintage Bus Route 100. Withdrawn from passenger service in 1946 it was numbered 693J and served as the canteen at the Windmill Road, Greenford terminus. It was based at Alperton garage from 1947 to 1953 where it is seen in this photograph taken on 3rd May 1952. After a short period with British Road Services it was disposed of to Rush Green Motors where it remained slowly deteriorating until rescued in 1966. (A.B. Cross)

The corner shop was an ideal location for cinemas in the locality to place boards to advertise the current programmes. This is another example of something, once very commonplace, becoming extinct. TD32 on the long established local Upminster route 248 picks up a few passengers while a family cross smartly over the road in the background in front of some old style "keep left" bollards. (J. Gascoine collection)

Battersea's RTL375 is seen passing tidied up bomb damage, still awaiting the attention of the property developer, in Theobalds Road. Front advertisements for the Motor Show at Earls Court are carried on the bus while the roadside notice board is dedicated to the Borough of Holborn Road Safety Campaign. Doubtless that campaign will be greatly helped later in the year when the tram tracks are removed. Notice in the foreground the poor state of the granite setts in which the tracks are laid. (S.E. Letts)

The leading bus photographed at Buck Street, Camden Town is RTW148 when garaged at Putney Bridge. Route 74 provided the service to London Zoo for very many years and the second vehicle in this line up is a Chalk Farm RTW doubtless working the supplementary shuttle to Baker Street which catered for the traffic to this attraction.

(J. Gascoine collection)

East Grinstead received four RLHs in October and November 1952 although vehicles of a lowbridge configuration were not essential to the operation of their routes. Here RLH44 works through Horley on the 424 route beside William Whitmore's delightfully old fashioned corn merchant's shop. This was the bus which in 1970 was to be converted by London Country Bus Services to a mobile uniform store with the fleet number 581J and as such is now preserved. (A.B. Cross)

Park Street, Luton on the 1st June provides the setting for STL491 transferred into Luton from Grays four months earlier. The 360 route shuttled back and forth from Luton to nearby Caddington village for many years. In the background an RT lays over before the trip to rather more distant Rickmansworth on route 321. (A.B. Cross)

A somewhat grim faced queue at Sevenoaks Bus Station watches the photographer as STL407 slinks round the corner to travel just down the road to Tubs Hill Station, more correctly known as Sevenoaks (Tubs Hill) Station. The 454 route was to receive an allocation of RTs later in the year but this is 26th March and the STL still gives good service. The days of the disposable Biro had not yet arrived either as shown by the remarkably clean advertisement on the rear of the bus. (A.B. Cross)

The 477 route was another Country Area service to receive RTs during the year under review. Here Swanley Junction's RT3436 takes passengers on board in Dartford before heading off to Crockenhill. (A.B. Cross)

A small number of unrebuilt single deck LT class vehicles had to soldier on until the end, which came with the arrival of the new Central Area RF class. Photographed here at Crystal Palace on the 20th April, LT1114 was renovated in the winter of 1944/5 by Sunny Doors Ltd. of Southend on Sea and the reformed rear profile, just visible in this picture is more clearly shown in a rear view of the vehicle elsewhere in this book. (J.H. Aston)

The unique G30, which had been rebodied by Northern Coachbuilders, was shown in the 1951 book operating on route 79. It continued in service from Alperton garage until July 1952 but here on the 14th January it has paid a visit to Chiswick works for some now forgotten reason. It is parked outside the canteen building in the complex, now regrettably completely obliterated. (J.C. Gillham)

An interior shot of the Argent Street garage at Grays on its last day of operation. In the line up from left to right are STL491, RT4124, STL731 and RT4099. A photograph of the latter vehicle returning to the garage shortly before this picture was taken is seen elsewhere in the book. (A.B. Cross)

RTW267 is seen on route 11 to Shepherds Bush negotiating Parliament Square at speed, judging by the angle of the body to the rear wheel. The vehicle is one of a number used on this well known route from Riverside garage. The advertisement for shredded wheat is a little less macho than recent publicity for this breakfast cereal. (R. Marshall)

The Dagenham Council appear to have successfully completed a pruning exercise to the roadside trees in this view taken just off Heathway at Dagenham. RTL479 operates the Sunday 139A route to Chigwell Row, which must have been more pleasant than the stark regimental air of these trees and the Becontree Estate. (J. Gascoine collection)

This view of D141 shows very clearly the fluted top to the Daimler radiator with the legendary London Transport plate nicely placed in the middle. At this time route 32 ran between St. Helier Avenue and Raynes Park with certain journeys extended to Worcester Park Station during the rush hours. (Lens of Sutton)

The temporary repairs to war damaged Southwark Bridge, still in situ in 1952, are negotiated by RT3843 from Brixton on Route 95 on 30th April. In the background is the steeple of St. Michael Paternoster Royal, one of the many City churches burnt down in the Great Fire of London, rebuilt by Wren and receiving bomb damage in the Second World War. The unusual name does not signify regal patronage but is said to be a corruption of La Reole, a place near Bordeaux from which local vintners once imported wine.

On New Year's Day RT4099 crosses the long removed level crossing by Grays Station as it heads back to the garage at Argent Street after operating the former Eastern National route 45 between Grays and Linford. Next day the full blind apertures will be properly used and Linford will be served by route 380. This particular vehicle was transferred into Grays from Guildford for the route changes but a month later returned to its less industrial home. (A.B. Cross)

Still pristine new, apart from having acquired a taste for Booth's gin - and why not? - Weymann bodied RT3458 passes its initial Watford High Street home on the way to Oxhey Estate on 27th March. This was one of the vehicles to be transferred to the new Garston garage when it opened on 18th June. (A.B. Cross)

On the 10th May, RTL276, caught partially in the shadows of London Road, Enfield, journeys to Lower Edmonton on route 128, destined to become W8 some seventeen years later. RTLs were comparatively short lived at Enfield garage, being displaced by new RTs between May and September. Those remaining during the summer tended to be allocated to this particular route. As displayed on so many buses of this period, just about every air operator would have liked to take you to various destinations around the globe, and here it is the turn of extinct BEA by way of their Silver Wing service. (A.B. Cross)

One of Muswell Hill's new RF buses, RF290, pauses at the Jack Straw's Castle stop on Hampstead Heath on its way to Golders Green. A new style of blind for Central Area single deck routes was introduced with the new RFs. Identical to the final type of restricted blind used on double deck routes, it only gave two intermediate points alongside a rather larger route number instead of being alongside the route number. The plate above the entrance displaying the route number was unique in the RF family to the Central Area buses. (J.G.S. Smith collection)

RF107 is seen at the Minories Bus & Coach Station, Aldgate. This particular RF was delivered to Grays garage in December 1951 along with a batch that totalled nineteen, replacing the TF class coaches which hitherto had operated service 723. In turn Green Line RT class buses ousted the short lived RF allocation on this route in June 1954. (S.E. Letts)

Trees in summer foliage at Esher Road, Hersham on the 24th May provide the background for T32. This bus dates from December 1929 since when it has had its entrance moved from rear to front, been rebuilt by Marshalls of Cambridge and received an oil engine. The weight restriction on Walton Bridge ensured the survival of these veterans for use on route 218. (J.C. Gillham)

An interesting interior view of a 5Q5 type of body, in this case belonging to Q109. The similarity of this 1936 Park Royal built body to the 1952 Central Area RFs is most striking. The offside longitudinal seating for six persons was placed above the engine compartment giving a warm ride to passengers on an overworked bus. The decor is typical late 1930s style and of particular note are the window winders placed at the top of the frame. The entrance right forward of the saloon is a common enough feature on modern vehicles but when these were built was something of a novelty. The fare board is placed somewhat inconveniently between the entrance and the driver's compartment, a situation rectified in the RF design by putting it above the windscreen. (J.C. Gillham)

The date is the 3rd August and Duple bodied D89, working as AL13 on route 77A, sits in the sunshine whilst one of the crew stands on the platform. The curtained shop front to the right of the vehicle is the Terminus Cafe, doubtless well patronised by the crews of route 77A. (J.H.Aston)

Red STL1896 seen at Slough working the 444 route from Slough to Windsor with the standard wartime Country Area blind display. In this case the information is even less than usual since a double-ended 'lazy' blind is in use. (Geoff Morant)

On the 3rd August D47 waits to commence another journey on route 118 from Raynes Park to Clapham Common (Old Town). Five opening windows are now fitted in place of the original two provided when delivered on this particular batch of Brush bodied 1/1D3s. The ventilators fitted at the front helped distinguish these earlier Ds from Duple bodied examples which only had plain windows fitted.
(J.H. Aston)

Park Royal bodied G151 is seen in Southbury Road, Enfield on the 15th March. The bus now wears the current livery of all over red with one cream band between decks, a far cry from its original livery of brown and yellow ochre with pinkish brown roof worn when first delivered to the Board in July 1945. Operating route 135, Forty Hill to Brimsdown - a name which somehow fitted this area of power station cooling towers and factory chimneys - the bus spent most of its operating life at Enfield garage, which it has just passed. (J.C. Gillham)

For some unknown reason six red RTLs were allocated to the Country Area in December 1951, all being moved into Barking very early in 1952. Here, on the 9th January, RTL1252 operating from Hertford garage waits for a crew change at Fairfax Road before depositing its passengers in Hertford. This was a regular experience, somewhat maddening if you were in a hurry to get the shopping done but these travellers look fairly phlegmatic about the delay. (A.B. Cross)

When the new Norbiton garage opened on the 14th May it assumed much of Kingston's work including the 213 route to Belmont Station. They also continued the Kingston practice of borrowing some 5Q5s for Saturday work, usually from Sidcup. Here Q178 starts out down Clarence Street on its journey with a fine load. (A.B. Cross)

STD25 is seen on the forecourt of Enfield garage ready for a trip on Excursion 33 to London Airport. Behind can be seen the turning circle wiring for trolleybus 649. Advertising is carried by the STD for the Golden Arrow, the Southern Region's exclusive all Pullman rail service to Paris and is a reminder of the prestige continental travel not yet completely lost by the railways. (A.B. Cross)

The date is the 19th July and G432 is photographed in High Street South, East Ham. The bus was a long-stay resident of Upton Park garage. It is interesting to compare this Park Royal built body of 1946 origin with RT class bodies built at the same factory and delivered only fifteen months later. Such comparison demonstrates the definition of the word "utility" as applied to bus bodywork! The front advertisements promote the boat trips available from North Woolwich to Southend and Margate which were popular excursions at the time. Unfortunately this bus is only going as far as the Royal Albert Dock. (J.C. Gillham)

What a difference a livery makes! G333 (HGC112) at the same place on the same day as identically bodied G432 (HGC211) above, carries the contemporary 1952 paint scheme and although some may say it was a more drab livery, the vehicle could be said to have taken on a moderner appearance. (J.C. Gillham)

Newly delivered RT3527 works the East Grinstead route 428 on 6th June. Later in the year East Grinstead garage received some RLHs to cover this route although as evident here such low-height vehicles were not necessary and must have appeared to be a retrograde step to regular upper-deck passengers. (A.B. Cross)

Route 312 which had long been associated with the Gammons Lane area of North Watford was re-routed on 5th March at Market Street in Watford to run to Langley Way in Cassiobury Drive, replacing the 332 route on this stretch of road. Here Watford High Street's RT1032, which has received full blinds, pauses outside the garage for a crew change. (A.B. Cross)

The confusion that arose when the "frying pan" shaped tram services 8 and 20 between Victoria, Streatham and Tooting were replaced by buses 57 and 57A was resolved on 14th May by renumbering the 57A, which ran to Streatham via Clapham and Tooting, to 181. Still displaying its "VIA CLAPHAM" route blind, so necessary when numbered 57A, RTL955, working from Clapham garage, is at Tooting Bec. (C. Carter)

You could be forgiven if you did not realise that this body of LT494 was at the time being used as a chicken house, a sort of forerunner of the present battery house in which most chickens are reared nowadays. The chassis was fitted with a lorry body for farm use and both could be seen on a farm at Ferny Hill near Cockfosters. Although this is an LT5/7 body the roof has lost its route number box which was the outcome of it being stuck under the low bridge in Stroud Green Road at Finsbury Park. (R. Hobbs/A.B. Cross)

Elsewhere in this book you will find some pictures of Melsbroek Airport in Belgium which was just beginning to develop to meet the needs of post-war air travel. Similarly London Airport was growing at Heathrow although still very primitive. On the 12th March Uxbridge garage received an extra T to cover additional journeys on route 222 between Uxbridge and "London Airport North" i.e. the huddle of temporary buildings along the Bath Road which served the airport at the time. Here T750 covers one of these workings at Uxbridge.
(D.A. Ruddom collection)

During the year under review Edgware garage lost its allocation of RTLs in favour of RTs and on the 15th June RT3339 stands on the forecourt of Edgware Station while operating route 141 to Borehamwood. This is another photograph which led the compilers to believe that 1952 was not a particularly good summer although subsequent research revealed that there was a heatwave in London in July. (A.B. Cross)

Standing in Station Road, Sidcup at the bus stop which purports to be only for route 228, Q180 is seen taking on passengers for a short working to Blackfen (Woodman) on the 241 route. When first commissioned Q180 was a Country Area bus and was unique in being the only 5Q5 delivered new to Northfleet garage. (A.B. Cross)

Pictured near New Cross, its new home garage, RT5 works tram replacement route 177 on the 7th July. The new route blinds issued to New Cross for route 177 and 182 were of an experimental nature containing only three places in a larger type face. Whilst clarity might have been achieved, the intending passenger is left to guess whether the bus is going to reach the Embankment from New Cross via Old Kent Road or Camberwell Green. (J.F. Bearman)

This more unusual view of STL2477 shows how well the old and obsolete livery of red and white with black lining and brown roof was carried along the side and rear of the bus. Having appeared in May 1950 and delicensed in December 1953, it carried on its career with London Transport for a few months longer from March to November 1954, first as a staff bus and later as a trainer, before being disposed of to Bee Line for operation in and around West Hartlepool.

STL616 slowly attracts business while standing in the bus station at Hertford waiting to commence a further journey on route 327 to Nazeingwood Common. Normally green STLs used the route number box together with a two line display. For some reason this STL has the Central Area masking arrangement which has produced this odd result. Fortunately the journey to Nazeingwood Common ran via Broxbourne Station. (Lens of Sutton)

This view was taken on the 6th July, which was the first day of operation of tram replacement route 163, and shows STL474 with typical South London housisng which has escaped the ravages of war. The driver, presumably a former tram man, appears to be about to pull sharply away from the kerb, one hopes not to the detriment of the oncoming cyclist. (A.B. Cross)

It took a long while for the re-organised Grays routes to settle down, indeed some may contest that they never have, and as early as 30th April the first of many further changes occurred. Route 328A (Purfleet to Woodside Estate) was renumbered 315 to allow for a new 328A between Aveley and Purfleet. Here RT1061 works the renumbered route carrying a side advertisement that might lead to confusion if the bus ever performed as a Green Line relief on the 723 route. (A.B. Cross)

This delightful photograph of C14 at Westerham was taken on 19th April. The country town atmosphere is heightened by the pillion rider with goggles and soft cap, the discreet signwriting of the still independent Westminster Bank and the cars nosed into the kerb. The only touch of modernity is the RLH on route 410. (J.H.Aston)

Bleak Hertford bus station on a wintry day provides the resting place for red STL1932, a 4/9STL14 variant which spent a year at Country Area Hertford garage before moving on to St. Albans garage as a trainer. The bus is operating on route 395 which, as now, provided the local service between the adjacent towns of Hertford and Ware. At this time 395 ran to Fanshawe Crescent while it was 395A which served Fanham Common. The small white building behind the bus housed a cafe much frequented by bus crews and spotters on days such as this one. (L.T.P.S.)

The auxiliary drawing office building of Chiswick works provides the backdrop here to 440W, originally T167 and converted to a 7 ton low "drop-side" lorry during 1940. Seventeen of the 7T7 sub-class were converted to lorries. These Green Line coaches had been transferred to bus work upon the delivery of the 10T10 variant in the late nineteen thirties. (J.C. Gillham)

Heading through Peckham, newly overhauled STL343 shows off gleaming paint work and air pick up scoop in the front dome for the ventilation system. Only twenty five bodies were so equipped with this device when built, although many provincial operators specified such a fitment on their vehicle when new. (A.B. Cross)

This is the sort of tantalising view inside Reigate garage that could be gained by intrepid bus spotters in 1952. On the 19th May from alongside Q186, one of the two 4Q4 vehicles delivered six months after the rest of the class, ST1089 can be seen with CR17 visible through the lower deck windows. The CR was to move on in the following month to Tring garage for passenger use. One of the Inter-Station Cs can be seen through the driving cab area of the ST while a further example of the CR class lurks in the shadows to the left. (D.W.K. Jones)

RTL1029 on route 161 which became involved in the final tram replacement programme. Prior to June 1952 it was basically Eltham to Chislehurst with peak projections at one end to Sidcup and at the other end as a limited stop service to Woolwich. In June however this latter section became a daily stopping service partly replacing the trams over Woolwich Common. (John Gascoine collection)

The extensive buildings of Windsor garage, redolent of the optimism of the young LPTB in the mid thirties, are now regrettably no more. This looks like a Sunday or Bank Holiday and passengers "in the know" have felt it worth the ten to fifteen minute walk from the town to the garage to enable them to board an empty bus instead of taking their chance on the queues in the town centre. STL1927 performs as a "RELIEF" on route 441, working a short journey to the Crown at Slough. (L.T.P.S.)

Westbound buses on the Victoria Embankment used the reserved tram track which resulted in a tight squeeze when east bound trams were encountered. It also gave rise to a road sign at Blackfriars with the amusing legend "Buses Only On Tram Tracks". Here, a week before the end of the trams, Clapham's RTL853 working on route 155, which replaced tram service 4 passes an ex LCC tram of class E/3, number 1970. The 38 with its sister service 36 would become bus 177 on 5th July. (A.B. Cross)

LT1113 was one of the last single deck LTs to be withdrawn from service. Although unrebuilt by Marshalls of Cambridge it was fitted with an oil engine in June 1950. Photographed here standing outside Wimbledon Southern Region Station it is presumably on a rail replacement service since the only regular time that this forecourt was used for buses was during the Wimbledon Tennis fortnight and the weather suggests this is not likely! The bus was allocated to Sutton garage but it has obviously been lent to Merton for this duty. (A.M. Wright)

A contrast in body styles is shown here in South Street, Romford with red liveried T576 carrying LPTB bodywork being overtaken by a Westcliff on Sea AEC Regent still bearing its now disused roof route number box. While the T is merely trundling up and down in Romford, the Westcliff vehicle is nearing the end of its long run from that Thames estuary resort. (A.B. Cross)

On the 5th February STL439 complete with offside stencil for route 103 is pictured here at Romford Station. It is operating a "when working" journey and will turn off the normal line of route when it reaches Oldchurch Road to return to its garage at Hornchurch. 103 was the last route from Hornchurch garage to lose its Guys in May but obviously the replacing STLs made appearances in advance of this date. In its final form as shown here the bus was classified 2/16STL18. (A.B. Cross)

RTL1050 is nowadays preserved by David Thrower of Warrington in Cheshire. In the upper photograph the bus is seen in original condition on 22nd June operating route 82 from Athol Street garage, which was its first home when put into service in October 1950. It is destined for Rotherhithe (Brunel Road) to which it was extended on 14th May thereby chasing its tail, as it were, around the Surrey Commercial Docks area. The registration plate and brass London Transport identification plates fitted to the chassis of the preserved bus state that it is RTL1050 but closer examination of the Leyland identification plate reveals that the left hand side member at least originally belonged to RTL1060. Add to this the fact that on the vehicle's last overhaul at Aldenham Works in 1958 it received the body first carried by RTL1041 and you can appreciate the hybrid that is now thankfully preserved. The lower picture shows RTL1041 on the 2nd June in Glenthorne Road, Hammersmith, returning to Mile End from London Airport on one of the numbered excursions introduced in 1952. (A.B. Cross)

With the spire of St. Anne's, West Hill, Highgate, immortalised by its proximity to Sir John Betjeman's childhood home, in the background, Q225 pauses at the Jack Straw's Castle stop on Hampstead Heath. Immediately behind the gents enjoying a chat on the seat is the Vale of Health, site of the famous Bank Holiday fairs. The panelling on the bus carrying the fleetname clearly shows the minimum amount of work carried out to re-commission these green painted vehicles for Central Area duty. (Lens of Sutton)

Although the Festival of Britain was removed from the South Bank after 1951, the Festival Gardens and Fun Fair at Battersea Park remained for several years and here, at the south end of Chelsea Bridge, RTL400 disgorges its load of pleasure seekers on the shuttle service re-introduced for the summer from Sloane Square Station. (C. Carter)

The date is the 14th September and parked at the Colchester garage of Eastern National Omnibus Company are at least two of the buses used by London Transport on the routes taken over in the Grays area in 1951. Six of these 1936 built Bristol JO5G models fitted with Eastern Counties dual purpose 31 seater bodywork were originally on temporary loan to the Executive. Nearest the camera is 3628, registered DEV464, while standing next to it is 3631 (DEV467). (J.C. Gillham)

On the 24th April at Kingston T298 lays over on route 216 with Kingston railway station and the completed chimney of the power station in the background. This vehicle is an 11T11 which class comprised 1931 chassis and more modern bodies transferred from R class buses in October 1938. Not many of the class survived long enough to receive the style of livery this bus carries. (J.C. Gillham)

D84 carries a good number of passengers as it pauses at Tooting Broadway to pick up more on its way to Mitcham. The trams last ran here in January 1951 and as a temporary measure the running rails in the foreground have been tarmaced over while the conduit slot remains. (C. Carter)

As the second batch of 56 RLH class buses made their debut during this year, it was possible to withdraw the last members of the ST class, which were all lowbridge variants. In this view of the upper deck of an ex-National, Short Brothers bodied ST, the gangway either side of the seating is clearly shown. The single skinned side and roof are of note as too are the ceiling mounted light bulbs. By the time this photograph was taken at Chiswick Works the seats had been re-upholstered in standard post-war RT type moquette. (J.C. Gillham)

With the famous Royal Small Arms Factory at Enfield Lock as a backdrop, STD72 waits to depart on a journey to the Arkley Hotel at Barnet on route 107A. A number of these splendid vehicles were transferred to Enfield from Hendon in February 1952 after they had been displaced by RTLs on route 13. In their turn they replaced Enfield's Guys on the 107/107A despite being eight or nine years older. The news vendor's kiosk carries some very substantial advertisements for such a temporary structure. (C. Carter)

Two learner vehicles parked side by side. STL2678 sports the Country Area green livery of its former duties, being one of a small batch of oil engined, crash gearbox variety delivered new in 1941/2. The coding of this vehicle was always 17STL17/1, the original body never being separated from its original chassis. RT140 wears the then current Central Area red livery and makes an easily recognisable different approach to body design when the two buses are compared. The slightly later STL17/1 bodies were in fact to wartime specification and were cloned from the pre-war STL designs produced by Chiswick Works. (J. Gascoine collection)

In this view of vehicle free Dartford Market Place STL2138 stands with H1B class trolleybus 786B on the erstwhile 696 route to Woolwich. This was one of the vehicles rebodied by East Lancs following war damage. The STL is working a short journey on 423 to Lane End, which incidentally has acquired a mysterious plural version on the blind. This road now forms part of the one-way traffic system through Dartford town centre.

(Lens of Sutton)

Q33 is seen inside East Grinstead garage parked perilously close to one of the well marked and protected pillars supporting the roof. Behind is a 10T10 coach, neither vehicle being required for immediate service. The date is 5th March and in just a little over a year the Q would be dismantled by the LTE for scrap. (A.B. Cross)

RTL1281 operating from Walworth garage on tram replacement route 185 to Blackwall Tunnel via Dulwich and Lewisham. The setting is Vauxhall Bridge Road at Victoria, confirmed by the Ian Allan Ltd. sign placed high on the building to the left announcing their old shop, below street level, which was the mecca for all transport enthusiasts visiting the area at the time.

On the 28th June TF55, still in Green Line colours but now carrying a London Transport fleet name, stands in Park Street, Luton about to perform on the pleasant journey over to Flamstead village, just inside Hertfordshire. During 1952 deliveries of the Green Line batch of RF class coaches were completed and many changes occurred in the use of former Green Line coaches as one will see throughout this book. (A.B. Cross)

An interesting view of Epping garage forecourt with STL773 about to start a journey that isn't clear from the indicator. It is assumed the passengers already on board are trusting regulars who know how far up the A11 it is going to go! The other buses in the picture are all of the RT class which Epping had first received in November 1948. RT1017, farthest from the camera has had its ultimate blind aperture commissioned but still needs the route number box unmasking for a full blind display. Unvandalized route information boards, one of the stone or concrete style of telephone boxes and Shell and BP fuel signs complete the picture. (C. Carter)

The parking lot at Edgware garage was usually full of new RT/RTL vehicles awaiting tram conversions or withdrawn vehicles awaiting disposal but here three of Edgware's own vehicles occupy the ample space. From left to right TD92, 105 and 104 carry Mann Egerton 31 seat bodywork on Leyland Tiger PS1 chassis. (R.H.G. Simpson)

London Airport North was the original terminal area just off the Bath Road and, on the 27th July, it plays host to an impressive line up of vehicles. Nearest the camera, East Kent's CFN100, a Park Royal bodied Leyland PS1 with, moving through the line, green RT2503, red RT322 and 582. A Bedford OB breaks the line up of RTs but next to it stands RT4013 with an unidentifiable Park Royal bodied RTL to its right. This picture is almost akin to a modern day rally photo although the telegraph pole probably best identifies its age. (J.F. Bearman)

RFW8 is parked on the area reserved for London Transport buses and coaches at Whipsnade Zoo next to one of the specially finished Weymann bodied Green Line RTs from Romford garage, which has doubtless arrived on Route 726. The extensive use of glass on these private hire coaches gave a fine all round view to the passengers who used these high specification touring coaches. (J.G.S. Smith collection)

Turning on to Lambeth Bridge, STL436 is followed by one of the real classic British cars - a Wolseley - which were always distinguishable from other makes by having the manufacturer's name illuminated at the top of the radiator.

Red STL572 operates from Grays garage on route 349 which provided the service from Grays to the oil refineries of Coryton and Shell Haven, the most easterly point ever reached by a London Transport bus service. This vehicle finished its days with London Transport in September 1954 as a 2/16STL18 before moving on to W. North, the dealers of Leeds. (Lens of Sutton)

Forest Gate garage received a small number of the SRT class during the previous year transferred in from other garages. They settled down on to the 66 route from Leytonstone to Hornchurch. SRT14, which had run from Camberwell and then Holloway garages, would be one of the fortunates to receive an overhaul in March 1953 and this 1952 picture gives the impression it was not before time. (John Gascoine collection)

The imposing signs to the Southern Railway's Wimbledon Station, now of course at least five years out of date, form the backdrop to STL1223 operating on the special service for the Wimbledon Tennis Championships. Customised advertising adorns the STL as it also does the one in the background which has started on its journey to the famous tennis grounds. (Lens of Sutton)

Overhauled midway through the previous year, STL419 still makes a pleasing sight as it stands, almost posing for the camera, at the rear of Dunton Green garage while carrying blinds for the Orpington to Sevenoaks route 431. (Lens of Sutton)

Before the 14th May route renumbering RTL1074 stands at the Victoria terminus in Vauxhall Bridge Road ready for a journey on route 57A to Streatham (*via Clapham*) as the intermediate blind clearly shows. The following RT2030 is seen on the complementary route 57 to Tooting Bdy (*via Brixton*). This is the same 57 route as now works to Kingston from Streatham having moved bodily southwards over the years. (J.G.S. Smith collection)

The last 48 tram had run up Milkwood Road, Herne Hill on the 5th January and now on 20th July the road is being reinstated after the tracks have been removed. RTL1186 of Camberwell garage, its rear registration obscured by a warning flag (notice cones were not invented in 1952!), works the extension of long running route 42 which had replaced the replacement bus route 48 on Sundays, just four months after its introduction! The conductor stands in the customary place probably unaware that he has selected the incorrect destination. Aldgate was the end of the 42 route and therefore the word ONLY should not be shown. This display was obviously intended for Camberwell's route 40 which in 1952 travelled on to Wanstead.
(J.H. Price)

1952 was the last year of operation of the ST class of vehicle, though it must be admitted these were the few remaining of the lowbridge variety. Here, at Rayners Lane, green liveried ST141 works Central Area route 230, which required this type of vehicle due to the low bridge at Headstone Lane, which still claims an occasional victim. The longevity of this particular ST was due to the replacement lowbridge vehicles in the form of red RLHs not arriving until later in 1952 and was aided by replacement of its petrol engine with a diesel unit in December 1949. (V.C. Jones)

LT1203, shown in the 1948 book, is still with Billy Smart's Circus although the paint work is deteriorating four years later. This was one of only four such buses built using a LGOC CC type chassis with Meadows engine and LGOC bodywork. These four vehicles were an experiment in the use of a six wheeled vehicle at Chiswick Works. The body of this particular vehicle is of the LT5 variety with straight staircase and blind box built into the cab roof. In the period between these vehicles being designed and put into service AEC introduced three new types of passenger chassis, namely the Renown, Regent and Regal, which accounted for the fact that no more CC type were produced.

On 14th January red liveried STL1819 passes the Post Office in St. Peters Street, St. Albans as it sets out for Dunstable which it will reach via the old A5 road. One of the last pre-war STLs to be withdrawn from service in 1954 it then performed as a staff bus for eight months or so before making its way to Birds, the well known dealer of the time at Stratford upon Avon. (A.B. Cross)

Withdrawals of the austerity Guy Arab buses had started in 1950 and continued through to 1953, the last running in passenger service on Christmas Eve 1952 on route 101. G373 however was withdrawn early in 1951 from the London Transport fleet and by 1952 was operating for the Western SMT Company Ltd of Kilmarnock as their 991. It was to be rebodied with a new Alexander low height 53 seat body at the end of 1952 but it is seen here at Renfrew Ferry en route for Paisley with its original 1945 built Weymann body which has had its destination box revised to suit local practice. (Ian Maclean)

Athol Street, Poplar garage was unique in the Central Area in converting its blind displays to this "semi-restricted" layout utilising the route number box. STL832 shows this arrangement as it works the Rotherhithe Tunnel route 82. (W.J. Haynes)

Two pictures from the Sabena Airlines' archives appear in this book. Both were taken on the 18th October at what was then known as Melsbroek Airport. This site has since developed into the Brussels International Airport now known as Zaventem. The leading bus was originally G35, a Weymann bodied example, while the following one, although another ex-London vehicle remains a mystery. It is, however, from the Park Royal bodied batch numbered G72 to G136. It would appear that the buses are being used for some sort of guided tour. The peaked cap official in the top deck nearside seat seems to be giving a commentary using a hand held microphone although the bleak surroundings must have taxed his descriptive powers!
(Sabena Belgian World Airlines)

The RFW class were the most luxurious coaches to be operated by London Transport for a good number of years. Here RFW6, together with a further example, waits to take another party on board. Note the hinged passenger door which, unlike their LTC predecessors, precluded any thought of ever operating these vehicles as reliefs on stage carriage services. (R.H.G. Simpson)

The date is the 15th April and standing within the driver training area at Chiswick Works, dowdy G358 awaits its departure to W. North of Leeds later in the month. Careful inspection of this Massey bodied Guy, delivered to London Transport in August 1945, reveals few graceful curved lines, most unusual roof dome area and odd triangular corners to the rearmost upper deck window and above the platform. (J.C. Gillham)

Weymann bodied RT3950, first put into service from Norwood garage in October 1950, stands at Crystal Palace while awaiting its return journey to Golders Grn L.T. Station. Note the typical "dolly" type temporary bus stop, familiar to this day. (J.H Aston)

D170 stands alongside the railway at Raynes Park Station on the 3rd August. Delivered new in March 1946 as part of a batch of 37 Green Line Duple bodied vehicles in relaxed utility style it was classified 2/1D2/2. When replaced on Green Line duties by new RTs in 1950 they then moved into Merton garage and during 1951 were repainted into Central Area Livery. Many of them gained an overhaul in 1952 before being withdrawn from London service later in that year or the next. (J.H.Aston)

RLH9 pulls away from the Staines Western Region station in a slightly different view of this well known bus terminus, which appears several times in this series of books. Lurking in the background is a Twickenham garage STL waiting to take up duties on route 90 to Kew Gardens Station. (J.F. Bearman)

Seen at Raynes Park on Sunday 3rd August, Metro-Cammell bodied RTL909 rests before returning to Kings Cross on route 77A. Already the former tram garages are beginning to gain duties on long established bus routes and here Walworth provides a Sunday allocation on a route which dates back to 1917. The bus was originally delivered to Alperton garage in 1950 but subsequently was drafted into the vehicle store at Edgware before replacing trams at Walworth in 1951. (J.H. Aston)

By the year end all the Green Line variety of the new RF class of vehicles had been delivered to the Executive. Here, on the 8th March, Staines' RF163 waits at Gravesend to return across Central London on the 701 route to the more affluent destination of Ascot. (A.B. Cross)

The beginning of the end for the Daimler D class at Merton garage was signalled by the arrival in October of several RTLs, mostly secondhand, for use on route 49. The Leylands only remained at this shed a short while until a large influx of RTs took up the replacement programme in earnest. Here on the 12th October RTL918 with Metro-Cammell body waits on the peaceful and sylvan stand at Shepherds Bush Green. (A.B. Cross)

STL549 was pictured in the 1950 book operating on route 24 from Chalk Farm garage and now it is seen at London Bridge Station working on route 7A to East Acton, Goldsmiths Arms, from Middle Row garage. During the intervening period the bus has received an overhaul at Chiswick Works and a comparison between the two photographs will show that the style of bodywork, although the same, looks very different now that it sports the newest colour scheme. The sign on the lamp post indicating the prescence of Boots the Chemist is a little unusual. (A.B. Cross)

Luton's STL2147 is seen at the stop outside St. Albans garage with the familiar background of houses and St. Peter's Church. The date is 1st June but summer is a little late coming judging by the apparel of the group at the bus stop. (A.B. Cross)

Forty 10T10 class vehicles were repainted from green to red livery between August 1951 and February 1952 and in the process had their heaters and ashtrays removed. These repaints, together with some unrepainted green examples, were then used at many of the Central Area garages which operated single deckers. Here T539, which gained its red livery in February, appears to have taken on a full load at Ealing Broadway and patient ladies wait for the next 211 while the gentlemen seek to delay the driver with conversation. (Omnibus Society. C.F. Klapper)

Having been in store since the latter part of 1951, Q211 makes a welcome return to earning its keep, albeit in very different surroundings to that enjoyed earlier. In March 1952, due to repeated complaints by both passengers and staff about the poor condition of the single deck LT class vehicles based at Muswell Hill, twenty four of these magnificent looking 6Q6 type coaches were transferred in. They worked in Green Line livery from MH on routes 210, Golders Green to Finsbury Park and 244, Winchmore Hill to Muswell Hill Broadway where this picture is taken. They were replaced in October by delivery of the first of the Central Area RF class vehicles. The only alteration given to these Qs for this work was the substitution of London Transport fleetnames in place of the previously carried Green Line. (D.W.K. Jones)

Guildford Bus Station, Farnham Road, before the days of GS and subsequent Tillingbourne operation on route 448. C69 takes on passengers for a lovely little ride to the beautiful Surrey countryside around Newlands Corner, Gomshall and Peaslake. This vehicle had been lent to W.T. Edwards of Lydbrook, Glos. for three months during the war. It was to finish its passenger service at Guildford, being withdrawn in December 1953. However, a further 17 months was to elapse before it went to the Leeds dealer, W. North Ltd.

Red liveried Q8 unloads its passengers in Cromwell Road, Kingston before running through Kingston garage to undertake another journey on route 219 to Weybridge Station. (J.C. Gillham)

On 22nd October the 229 route was extended from its terminus at Wren Road in Sidcup to Bexleyheath Trolleybus Depot opening up a new link across south-east London. Sidcup garage received some additional STLs for the purpose and here STL1779 waits at the southern terminus of Orpington Station accompanied by a Bromley RT on route 61. (A.B. Cross)

Guildford garaged Q195 seen in the Onslow Street bus station of its home town on the 15th January. This vehicle was another casualty of the deliveries of Green Line RF coaches during the year but here it is working a short town journey to Burpham on the long Staines route 436. (A.B. Cross)

Sunday road works in the City on the 18th May were probably the cause of route 9 being diverted via narrow Lombard Street from which RTL386 is emerging. An interesting couple of cars follow as the bus passes one of the public subways to Bank Underground station. (A.B. Cross)

It is a warm 6th of July and the driver has opened the cab vent and windscreen of STL751, which stands on the forecourt of Morden Underground station. There must have been a shortage of blinds at Sutton garage as á side blind is fitted in the front box but since the 156 route was circular it is a reasonable compromise. (A.B. Cross)

STL2562, one of the small number of 15STL vehicles not to be converted to SRT configuaration, waits with RT4038 on the now fully integrated routes in Grays. A standard GY garage plate is now carried by the vehicles since the Argent Street premises have been closed as an operational garage and all duties are now operated from the Executive's own base in Hogg Lane. (L.T.P.S.)

For the final stage of tram replacement, which had been brought forward and took place on the 5th/6th July, some STLs were used and this meant that full blind displays returned to the STL class. Here at New Cross Station STL443, itself only slightly younger than some of the trams it replaced, shows the display for the 163 route which replaced the 40 tram between Embankment and Woolwich and was projected to Plumstead Common. (C. Carter)

A quiet moment on a Sunday at Morden Underground station, the southern extremity of the Northern Line and two STLs await their respective departure times. STL646 waits to take up duties as rostered A8 on the circular route 156, while in the background STL801 is soon to make the country journey down to Dorking LT Bus Station. The bodies carried by both the buses are of the STL5 variety, built by the LPTB in the mid-30s. Looking at the lady's millinery on the top deck of the 156 one wonders if the advertisement should have read "*Got* it at Harrods"! (R.G. Bristow)

Although starting on the same day, 14th May, as the new Norbiton garage opened, new route 265 was initially worked by Turnham Green garage. Here on the second day of operation RT2606 heads across London Road from Fairfield West at Kingston on its way to East Acton. A 65, which would follow it all the way to Kew Bridge, is not very far behind. (A.B. Cross)

Pre-war STL2070 heads a line up of post-war RT family buses in this view taken at the temporary terminus north of Hammersmith Bridge on the 19th July. The slip board beneath the front nearside bulkhead window announces that the bus is running to "Hammersmith Bridge Only". The present day problems with this bridge are nothing new and in 1952 it was completely closed to traffic from 9th July to 22nd August inclusive for repairs. On this occasion passengers were required to walk over the bridge and join the buses operating the southern sections of the routes from Castlenau. Admittedly the compilers of this caption are not noted alcoholics but neither can recall "Otard Brandy" which the bus tells us to ask for! (A.B. Cross)

The SRT class was still intact during the year under review and was only operated by a small number of garages. Here we have SRT86 operating from Cricklewood garage on route 16, a route accustomed to the unique sounds of this class for much of its life in passenger service. The chassis of this bus was once STL2597. Route 16, as now, provided the backbone of the service up the southern half of the Edgware Road. At the route's full extent it ran to Sudbury Town Station but there were many short workings as seen here with SRT86 bound for Neasden (Dog Lane) followed by the next bus to Cricklewood Broadway. (C. Carter)

STL491 was repainted green in November 1951 and in the book for 1950 it can be seen wearing its former red livery whilst working route 118 at Morden. Having moved to the Country Area in line with its new colours, it is seen here on the 31st May at Rickmansworth while carrying WA garage plates although officially allocated to Luton at the time. Unusually it carries a destination blind over the platform which may have escaped the notice of the conductor since he has not yet changed it. It is to be hoped he will make a better job of it than his efforts on the front blind! (A.B. Cross)

The Kingston area in south west London provided the enthusiast with many delights during this period. Within this book are a number of photographs showing the diversity of single deck buses which then operated from Kingston garage. If these are added to those shown in previous books, one can see why this acted as a magnet to the observer of the London Transport scene. Here we see green liveried T531 on the 26th April, temporarily borrowed from Leatherhead garage, in Wood Street, being followed by an original Morris Minor series MM introduced in 1948. (J.C. Gillham)

This picture of STL1973 at Rayners Lane on route 230 clearly shows some of the problems encountered on a low height bus body when fitted to a standard chassis, well before the Lodekka, Lowlander and Bridgemaster overcame the problem in later years. Passengers downstairs were accommodated in relative ease in the usual manner as long as you remembered to mind your head when standing up on the offside of the bus. Look closely however at the top deck where the seat backs are half way up the windows and passenger's heads are almost out of sight somewhere in the uppermost portion of the bodywork, giving you a permanent crick in the neck if you wanted to enjoy the view on a long journey. The normal height entrance/exit and driver's cab have been retained for obvious reasons. This STL, together with 19 others received these new STL19, 53 seater bodies during the war years replacing the original and older bodies.

Unlicenced red liveried CR43 seen parked at Epping garage on 14th August. Surprise, surprise - this particular CR gained green livery in May 1953 being afterwards sent to Leatherhead garage before being disposed of in December of the same year. (J.H. Aston)

Ex-Green Line Q213 working route 210 takes on a full load at the Archway Tavern for the climb up Highgate Hill on the 12th July. The tram tracks in the foreground, formerly used by service 35, have been temporarily filled with tarmac but have yet to be lifted. (J.C. Gillham)

STL1860 emerges from the southern portal of Blackwall Tunnel. It can easily be seen why specially roofed buses complete with tyres which had reinforced walls were considered a necessity. However, road works in the previous year to replace the granite setts and level the camber meant that by the time this photograph was taken normal roofed vehicles were allowable. The lack of white lines on what was still a two-way road is curious. For historians of London, "This tunnel was constructed by the London County Council and opened by the Prince of Wales on behalf of Her Majesty Queen Victoria on the 22nd May 1897 in the 60th year of her reign" is prominent on the stonework above the bus. (D.W.K. Jones)

(right) Additional width market lights were added to all the three buses which made the overseas trip to the USA and Canada. RTL1307, in its capacity as an information office and exhibition centre also had a ventilation grill neatly inserted on the rear nearside between decks area. This RTL, rather oddly, carried a Weymann body and was the first ever to do so. (Geoff Morant)

(below) Route 182 was introduced on July 6th to replace tram 46. Due to the fact that the last conversion of trams to buses, initially programmed for October, was brought forward to July and included in what was to have been the second to last scheme, sufficient numbers of new buses were not available. New routes 163 and 182 were thus interesting to the enthusiast in that STL buses were put to use on these routes, using full sets of blinds for the first time since the war years. Here STL1838, with an STL14 body, pauses in bomb damaged Upper Thames Street before turning on to the stand for five buses in Dowgate Hill at Cannon Street Station. The blind is set for a return journey to Eltham, Well Hall Station which, being short of the full route to Woolwich, displays the word "ONLY". This was a short lived style of the time. (John Gascoine collection)

Although repainted into bus livery Luton's TF53 still finds itself employed on its familiar duties on Green Line route 714. The tower of St. Peter's Church peers through the trees as the coach stops for passengers to alight at St. Albans garage. Substantial clothing is worn by most of the people in the photograph so perhaps the first day of June was not one of the warmer days of 1952. (A.B. Cross)

A policeman on point duty is necessary to supplement the traffic lights at Oxford Circus as two 13s vie for the lead down Regent Street. On the left Cricklewood's RT355 has been employed for some time on the route but new to the scene in this 19th January view is Hendon's RTL1295 on the right. Devotees of Hendon's STDs had a gloomy new year when these new Leylands began to replace the 1937 stalwarts. Worse was to come for Leyland enthusiasts however when three months later new AEC RTs removed the youthful Leylands from Hendon for use in other localities. (A.B. Cross)

The 1st June and TF26 stands opposite St. Albans garage partly in the shadow of a tree while operating on route 365 from Luton via "the lower road" to St. Albans and through to Hill End. This is another ex-coach transferred into St. Albans from Grays, in this case still carrying the two-tone green colours of Green Line but with London Transport fleet names. (A.B. Cross)

This was to be the last year of the austerity Guy Arabs whose guttural voices had shattered the peace of Romford and Hornchurch for some years. One of Hornchurch garage's replacement RTLs, 106 drafted in from Barking stops at Romford Station on the 26th June. Notice the incorrect spelling of Stapleford Abbotts on the blind, which was an error perpetuated by London Transport's compilers for some years. (A.B. Cross)

A nearside view of Q10 appeared in the 1951 book while operating on route 218. Here, still in green livery on the 26th April, it stands in Cromwell Road, Kingston about to drive through the garage and into the bus station before commencing another journey on route 215 out to delightful sounding Church Cobham. (J.C. Gillham)

The Hampstead Heath terminus of route 187 at South End Green provides the resting place for Craven bodied RT1475 working from Middle Row garage on 12th July. In line with all of these Craven built RTs which were the least standard of all the RT family members, it only lasted a short time in London service. In this case it was less than seven years before it was snapped up by Red Rover of Aylesbury as their number 1 and then spent another eight years in service on the north western fringes of the London Transport area. (J.C. Gillham)

A nice rear end view of CR4, clearly showing the filler cap to the cooling system and grill behind which was a rather large fan for a small engine. A 4.7 litre engine was fitted to these 20 seater buses. The vehicle stands on 14th August at the Green Man, Harlow working route 393 from Hoddesdon. (J.H. Aston)

The 16th July provides the photographer with the chance to catch STL670 as it stands alongside some partially completed shop development at Grays. I wonder what was being shown in the Co-operative exhibition which one was advised to be sure to visit? The appearance of the bus does credit to Grays garage who had to contend with notoriously messy roads in their operating area. (A.B. Cross)

STL2017 is seen here at Uxbridge Underground Station on 22nd July in company with a green liveried Mann Egerton bodied T in the background. The section of route 223 between West Drayton Station and Ruislip Station had been converted to double deck operation a year earlier but the section from West Drayton (Mill Road) to Uxbridge remained single deck due to the railway bridge at West Drayton. The lantern roof of Uxbridge Station is clearly seen in the background. Although still there today it now is incorporated into the new building of the garage and bus station shelter. (A.B. Cross)

A couple of STDs wait on the forecourt of Enfield garage to take up duties on the evening floodlighting tour, which commenced from Northumberland Avenue. This was one of the many innovations of the period which indicated some relaxation in the years of austerity which followed the war. (R.G. Bristow)

The very first local town service to serve Stevenage New Town was the 392 and it commenced on 26th March running between the White Lion in the Old Town to Monks Wood at Rockingham Way. Stevenage garage was still a twinkle in the eye and Hitchin garage could not accommodate double deckers, so Hatfield garage worked the route with a single RT. Here RT1097 lays over at the White Lion while behind T621 works a short journey on the 384 to Walkern. (A.B. Cross)

The gaunt shell of walls and towers of the bomb damaged Cannon Street Station loom beside RTL942 as it waits on the Dowgate Hill stand of tram replacement route 189A. It was only on a Saturday that this route reached Cannon Street, a reminder in itself that in 1952 the one and a half day weekend was still prevalent. (C. Carter)

An interior picture of T276, one of the 11T11 class, taken on the 27th May. The body is of Weymann manufacture seating 30 passengers in a front entrance configuration. Built in 1935 it was originally used to re-body an AEC Reliance chassis, fleet number R14, and was then transferred to its present Regal chassis in November 1938 when the Reliance was withdrawn. The pinch window openers betray the age of this remarkably modern and pleasant looking body. The central bell push in the rear bulkhead, highlighted by an arrow sticker, was a feature repeated on the 1952 Green Line RFs but the awkward side bell push above the window pillar was not. The last of these vehicles were withdrawn from Central Area service by the summer of 1952. (J.C. Gillham)

The highest numbered Q, 238, seen elsewhere in this book on its former Green Line duties, now works MH31 duty on route 244 in the autumn sunshine on the 23rd October. It pauses at the Southgate Station stop at the top of Winchmore Hill Road before the days when all buses circumnavigated the station buildings. (J.C. Gillham)

921LT, originally LT951, in its later role as a bus shelter carrier. A picture appears in the 1949 book of this series of the same vehicle when being used as a chassis frame mover and running on trade plate 041GT but in its later role it reverted to its original registration. (John Gascoine collection)

Two photographs of RTs taken on the 29th July in Watford High Street provide an interesting comparison of RT3 bodies, the upper built in May 1948 and the lower just five months later. Points of difference to note are the depth of the canopy valance, the nearside wing mirror and the canopy route number equipment. RT384 is a temporary loan. The 302 route had been extended to Adeyfield in February demonstrating the start of New Town development and RT384 will cover the new extension while RT965 performs a short working to Apsley (Shendish Lodge). (A.B. Cross)

Standing outside St. Albans garage on route 391, TF25 sports new Country Area bus livery. The date is 28th June and judging by the shadows it is probably early evening but there are still good loadings to be had for the run through Sandridge and Wheathampstead. This particular demoted coach was transferred to St. Albans from Grays upon the delivery of a large number of the new RF class to the latter garage. (A.B. Cross)

In this group of STDs on route 183 STD29, overhauled in 1950, is nearest the camera. This was one of those transferred out of Hendon garage to the Country Area on 1st September 1939 when most petrol vehicles were temporarily withdrawn and hurried diesel replacements had to be found. It operated from Luton and St. Albans garages but by the end of the month was stored and then returned to the Central Area to operate from Cricklewood garage until April 1941. The STD behind, which is still to be overhauled and lose its upper deck cream surround, experienced none of the wartime evacuation from Hendon. The location of this tightly packed corner is the Golders Green Station forecourt. (D.W.K. Jones)

(left) A nice frontal view of "Meccano Set" STL2477 within the confines of Alperton garage. Had the bus been given a roof mounted route number box, in the eyes of the author it would not have been too far removed from a standard STL in appearance. The cause of its nickname was the method of construction. Much of the body was simply pre-fabricated parts bolted together in conjunction with a normal STL roof and other components. Originally using restricted blinds, as seen on page 126 of the 1950 book, a full set of route blinds was carried during the latter part of its life. The lack of a separate route number box meant side blinds had to be used. This would have been neater if the destination box had been at the bottom as indeed it was on the rear. The 79A route was introduced on 6th August between Perivale and Edgware serving parts of Perivale and also the full length of Honeypot Lane for the first time.

(below) Waiting to commence the long haul to Dorking LT Bus Station, D178 is seen outside Morden Underground station which was opened in 1926. Nowadays, because of road improvements, buses stand in the opposite direction to that in which this D is pointing. The summer Sunday service to Dorking was a long standing duty which originated with the LGOC route 107 from Clapham Common which was subsequently renumbered 70 and then worked jointly by the LGOC and East Surrey, not to mention the independent operators of the 1920s. It continued as a joint Central and Country Area operation right up to 1938 and became part of route 93 in the following year. (R.G. Bristow)

(right) London Bridge station forms the backdrop to this picture of RTL376 as it is about to pull away from the stand to commence another journey on route 8A to the Lady Franklin at Old Ford on 22nd August. (A.B. Cross)

(below) The familiar half-timbered facade of the Royal Forest Hotel, Chingford provides the backdrop to T458, RTW77 and other buses long before the motor car ousted them from this delightful terminal. T458 received its red livery and internal modifications in November 1951 but the Green Line route board brackets remain. RTW77, delivered new in late 1949 to Shepherds Bush garage, was one of a large number transferred into Upton Park garage in July 1951 for their operations through Central London on route 15. Here it has strayed on to 145, which at the time was officially allocated RTs. (R.G. Bristow)

TF86 stands at New Barnet Station waiting to commence another journey on the rather tortuous 342 route which will wend through Potters Bar, Essendon, Cole Green and Hertingfordbury to Hertford before heading south again over Hertford Heath to Broxbourne.

According to the blind of Weymann bodied T750 it is working a shuttle on route 224 between Laleham and Staines via Worple Road. Many years after this photograph was taken the Ceylon Transport Board were the recipients of this particular bus, together with the vast majority of the post-war delivered Ts. (Lens of Sutton)

T536 clearly shows its T10 body with glazed partition to the right hand side of the entrance carried right up to saloon roof height. Compare this with the picture of a T10/1 body carried by T716 on page 78 of the 1948 book of this series. The bus, now finished in the then standard Central Area livery of all over red with the beading picked out in cream, is seen inside Kingston garage to which it was allocated on transfer from Country Area duties.

On the 20th February of the year under review the very first route of the complicated network of bus services which would serve Harlow New Town began. A seven minute journey westwards from the Green Man at Harlow Old Town took you along First Avenue to a point known as "Road E", in February likely to have been a mud bath. Here on 14th August the mud will have subsided although the qualifying description "New Town" is still adequate enough. Oddly, although the spur was off the main line of the trunk 396 route, no suffix was added to the route number at this stage. RT 1024 works the shuttle service. (J.H.Aston)

Pictured at the "Red Cross" stop in Reigate, 2RT2 RT124 works a weekend short working of route 410 as duty RG43 to Redhill. The sight of such a vehicle working in the Country Area inevitably caused much excitement among contemporary London bus enthusiasts and such a photograph would have been highly sought after. (Roy Hobbs)

Seen at Charing Cross operating route 11 to Shepherds Bush, RTW269 waits in the spring sunshine on the 18th May. Initially delivered to Edgware garage in the early months of 1950 for working suburban services, this bus, in common with a large number of the 500 strong class of vehicles, was reallocated to inner London duties during 1951. In this case, Riverside garage was the vehicle's new home including duties such as this on "prestige" route 11. (A.B. Cross)

RT1033 is standing outside Watford Junction railway station with the Clarendon Hotel as a backdrop. Delivered to Watford High Street garage at the end of 1948, the bus is still in its original livery. In this picture, taken on the 29th June, however, full blinds have now been fitted. The RT3/1 body was the first major body code change, brought about by the moving of the route number box from its position at roof level to between the decks and the addition of an illuminated route number box beneath the canopy. WA garage did not operate route 385 until the closure of WT twenty days before this photograph was taken. Also in the picture can be seen a Ford 8 Anglia and Ford 10 Prefect together with what appears to be a Lanchester saloon of mid 1930s origin. (A.B. Cross)

Two fine views of the inside of Inter Station Cub C107 give a good idea of the seating arrangement for 20 passengers in these deck and a half vehicles. The top picture is taken from the front of the saloon looking rearwards. To reach the rear raised portion of the coach meant a steep climb up steps with an even further step to your seat. As will be seen, the rearmost seat was only for 4 passengers and gave ample seating width. Once up the stairs one had a panoramic view from all quarters, including a view of the driver from a somewhat peculiar angle if so desired. Eight passengers were seated in the front portion of the vehicle while the other twelve enjoyed the better viewing in the raised section, the underneath of which was used for passenger's baggage. The bodies of these vehicles were metal framed and built by Park Royal, being finished to the usual pattern called for in 1936 by L.P.T.B. By 27th May 1952, when this picture was taken, all these vehicles were no longer operating but were in store at Reigate. (J.C. Gillham)

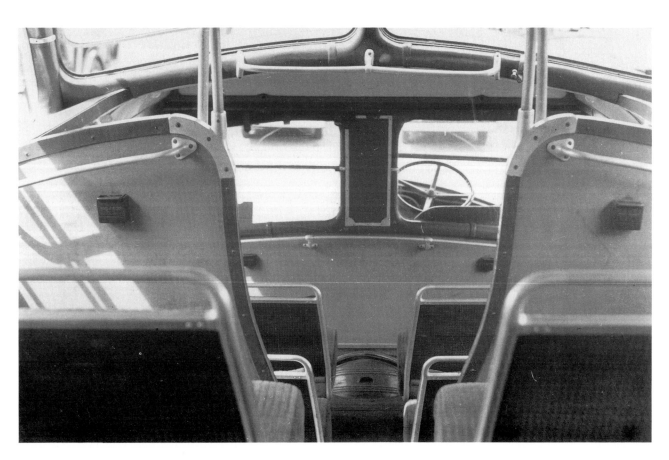

(*right*) The former RT97, converted to luxury Green Line coach RTC1, ended its days with London Transport allocated to Leatherhead garage for bus duties. These were usually on the 416 and 468 routes but here at Epsom Station on 25th May the bus has performed some sort of duty on route 408. This unique vehicle left London Transport in March 1955 when it was sold to the Leeds dealer W. North.
(J.F. Bearman)

(*below*) In this posed picture, RF289, the first of the Central Area red RFs is ready for entry into service on 11th September from Muswell Hill garage on route 210. Doors were still not acceptable to the Metropolitan Police and the omission of them gave the vehicles an oddly "London" flavour. Classified 2RF2 by London Transpsort, the Metro-Cammell bodies seated 41 and omitted the coach seats and luggage racks of the preceding 2RF2/1 class Green Line vehicles. In March 1956 this vehicle was one of six Central Area RFs to be converted to Green Line configuration and reclassified 2RF2/3.
(J.G.S. Smith collection)

Northfleet's Q59 is seen here just prior to its withdrawal and subsequent dismantling by the LTE in May. The bus waits in Gravesend for its next journey on route 489 to Ash (White Swan). As with many vehicles built up to the mid 1930s, side lights were incorporated into the bodywork, in this case above the windscreens. These lights were rather ineffective and were replaced with standard side lights but in this view the small rectangular plates used to cover the holes left when the lights were removed are just discernible. (John Gascoine collection)

An upper deck interior view of G107, a Park Royal variant but with a difference. Having been originally fitted with wooden slatted seating, it now sports the more familiar London Transport moquette, which it gained in July 1947. Of interest is the box shaped effect produced by these utility bodies and the primitive pinch type fitting to open the few windows so fitted. (J.C. Gillham)

Seen on the opposite side of the road to St. Albans garage on the 14th January, Q11 waits to continue its journey to Radlett on the 355 route. All 102 of this 4Q4 sub-class were delivered as country area buses, though during their years in service with London Transport many would see duties outside that for which they were originally intended. During 1936, only a few months after being put into service from Windsor garage, Q100, together with twenty six of its contemporaries, was converted for Green Line work and it is interesting to note that this coach was the last to revert to bus livery in the middle of 1948. By the middle of 1954 the vehicle was noted in use with the Electricity Authority of Cyprus, re-registered F520. (A.B. Cross)

The chassis of STL2649 is now seen in its new role as a distilled water tanker. The date is 26th September, which is only a month or two after the conversion had been carried out. 963J looks immaculate in its coat of green paint and is seen here parked within the Chiswick Works complex. (J.C. Gillham)

Excursion route number 5 (Circular Tour of London from Morden) utilising the delights of RT23. The date is 20th July and the bus is seen turning out of Parliament Square on what appears to be a rather warm day. Notice the white coated policeman on point duty, necessary since traffic lights were yet to be installed at this busy junction. (A.B. Cross)

A rather wet 2nd January and here in Gravesend C11 arrives on the rare route 492 from Kingsdown (Portobello Inn). At this time there were only two round journeys on this route on Monday-Friday mornings, a common enough pattern of frequency today but somewhat unusual in 1952. (A.B. Cross)

Orpington Station on the 18th May with C58 waiting to start another round of the circular route 471 through such delightful sounding villages as Cudham, Knockholt and Pratts Bottom. This latter name was once the source of great hilarity for the famous D.J. Tony Blackburn, no doubt to the annoyance of the inhabitants. The reverse direction blind to that shown here even went as far as to say "Pratts Bottom Circular" – but nobody told Mr Blackburn that! (J.H. Aston)

The arrival of the new Central Area lowbridge RLHs at the end of the year was none too soon and the two routes which at the time required such vehicles were prone to acquire any spare and usually antiquated vehicles they could from the Country Area. Very unusual indeed however was the appearance of former "Godstone" STL1048 at Merton on route 127. Here it approaches Morden Station with the Bell Punch equipped conductor in the doorway. Metropolitan Police regulations would have not permitted the use of the sliding door on such a route at the time and so perhaps he is doing his best to stem the draught.
(A.B. Cross)

STL1029 is parked neatly by the pond at Nazeingwood Common at the end of its journey on route 327 from Hertford via St. Margarets and Hoddesdon. Originally built by the Board as a front entrance 10STL6, this particular STL gained a standard rear entrance body in January 1948, receiving an overhaul in May 1951 which gave it this appearance which it kept till withdrawn from service in August 1954. (Lens of Sutton)

STL448 is seen waiting at Uxbridge station to perform on the circular tour of London (Excursion No. 6). Although the bus looks immaculate, one wonders what the riding qualities were like on an eighteen year old vehicle on such an arduous journey and why Uxbridge garage didn't offer their clients more comfort on one of their RTs.

Chalk Farm's RTL533 carries its original Park Royal body in this view of the bus at Crystal Palace on the 20th April. It was not until later in this year that RTL class overhauls commenced in earnest. How about popping over to Paris for 10 guineas (£10.50) or Nice for less than £30 as the front advertisements proclaim? (J.H. Aston)

The tram track and overhead wires at the West Norwood terminus remain undisturbed but unused as Stockwell garage's RTL1262 arrives on route 171 which had replaced tram 33 on the 6th April. The crowded blind describes the route taken in some detail. The line VICT.EMBKT KINGSWAY covers the devious route round Temple Place by which the buses gained the Kingsway and the last line shows the northward extension from Manor House through the virgin bus territory of St. Anns Road and Philip Lane to Bruce Grove at Tottenham. (C. Carter)

The interior of Weymann bodied G138 looking forward in the lower saloon provides some contrasts in design. The front bulkhead gives an air of austerity, the seating, with the screw on hand grips, a "provincial" look and the winding type windows set in pans a modern look. The heavily domed painted ceiling belies the vehicle's utilitarian origins. (J.C. Gillham)

T448, now demoted to staff bus duties and garaged at Reigate for the purpose, is seen here in the staff car park at Chiswick Works on 3rd April in company with other T class vehicles in the older style of livery. T448 had gained an overhaul in December 1950 resulting in its newer colour scheme. It was eventually to be disposed of to Harperbury Hospital at Shenley in Hertfordshire and was subsequently acquired for preservation. (J.C. Gillham)

Borrowed red RTL1090 stands in front of green liveried STL2292 while both operate the 410 route at Bromley North. The RTL is working the shorter section of route to either Westerham or Biggin Hill - the blind isn't clear on this point - and this short working will not reach the low bridge at Oxted. The blind display chosen however is for the opposite end of the route which would involve certain damage to this vehicle. This also raises the interesting question of how highbridge vehicles such as this, working from Godstone garage, reached the section of route which they were able to work north of the bridge at Oxted? (J. Gascoine collection)

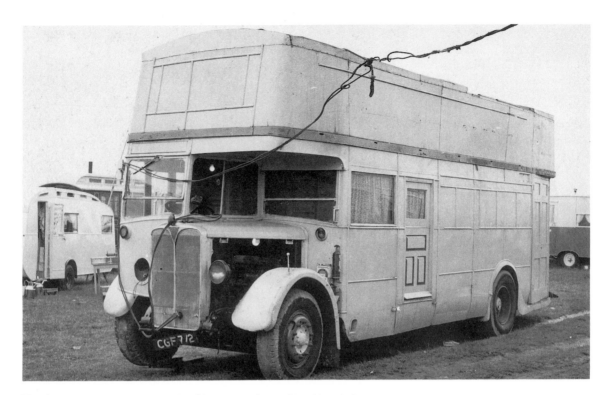

Until recent years many retired buses and coaches found their way into the hands of showmen who used them at fairgrounds and circuses. Such a fate obviously befell STL1985 although nothing else is known of this vehicle, apart from this picture, after it was sold to Daniels of Rainham in March 1951. (John Gascoine collection)

G436, Guy Motors' answer to the RT, still performs from Nunhead garage on the Peckham/Nunhead circular route 173. Later in the year, in the face of Union pressure, it was to move to Enfield who were to employ it on a similarly low profile route, the 121. (A.M. Wright)

In Green Line colours but with London Transport fleet name, T706 operates as NB12 on route 213 to Belmont Station on the 20th December. It is now seven months since the newly opened Norbiton garage replaced the Kingston garage workings on this route. The location is the Fountain Hotel at New Malden, a spot often favoured by the photographer. (A.B. Cross)

The first day of 1952 was the last day of the separate former Eastern National routes at Grays. Here on New Year's Day RT4l63, delivered new late in the previous year, has just passed STL1898, new in April 1937. Both are in Country Area green livery which the older bus only gained in November 1951, having previously been a Central Area vehicle, latterly at Leyton garage. The setting is the War Memorial in Grays and the 37A route ran to Tilbury Ferry by way of Chadwell St. Mary, while route 32B went via Blackshots Lane to Fairway (Long Lane) in the outskirts of the town just north of the By-pass; a journey of just 13 minutes. (A.B. Cross)

Tunbridge Wells coach station provides the resting place for STL419 while it waits to take up duties as a relief on Green Line route 704 to London;. This particular STL had gained its Country Area livery in June 1945 and kept it right through until its withdrawal from passenger service in February 1953. In earlier times the concrete posts had decorative metal work between them which was probably sacrificed in the interest of the war effort. The posts remain as a reminder of a bygone era. (L.T.P.S.)

Kingston Bus Station, now renamed Clarence Street Bus Station to differentiate it from the new upstart at Fairfield, with red liveried Q21 and T469 still wearing its Country Area green. They wait to take up duties on two of the several single deck routes which radiated from this suburban garage-cum-bus station. During the year under review the new Norbiton garage was opened and much of the normal day to day maintenance work passed there from Kingston. In this shot the buses appear to be standing crosswise in the Bus Station, suggesting that they were not running through the garage from Cromwell Road, which was the more usual practice. (D.W.K. Jones)

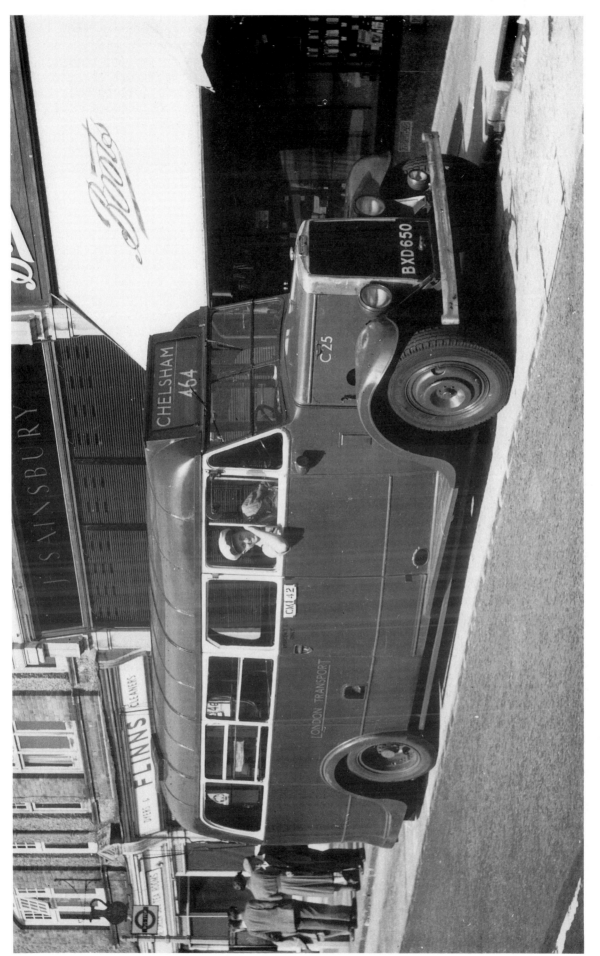

Station Road East at Oxted on Sunday the 17th August and the driver of C25 seems happy, whether because he was being photographed or returning to his garage is uncertain. The J. Sainsbury shopfront behind the Leyland Cub is of interest and although now occupied by different concerns, these shops are often still recognisable today. (J.H. Aston)

(left) It is the 24th May and at Bromley North, Godstone garaged STL2186 waits patiently for more business before setting off on route 410 which, if the bus is working through, will take it as far as Reigate. The lack of rear destination equipment on this wartime built lowbridge body means that from this angle one cannot tell its intentions. (D.W.K. Jones)

(below) Lovely looking old timer STL1055 is seen in its last year of operational service with London Transport complete with its 1951 overhauled and repainted bodywork in the contemporary style. Always classified 11STL7, being a mixture of an 8.8 litre engine with a crash gearbox, standard chassis of 1934 vintage and a Weymann low height 48 seat body, it, together with the other eleven vehicles which constituted the order, was known as a "Godstone" STL. Here it works from Addlestone garage having left its East Surrey home which gave its name to the class. For a couple of years after disposal by the Executive this particular STL could be seen operating for two different independents before finally being withdrawn from service in September 1955. (C. Carter)

(above) The quality of vehicle used on special services had improved immensely over the early post-war years as illustrated by this view of D6 and an RT on Epsom Downs. The rolling Surrey countryside and drivers dressed in their summer issue lightweight coats add to a scene repeated annually. (L.T.P.S.)

(right) Someone with a tidy mind decided during 1952 that it wasn't proper for main routes to be running with a suffix number while the parent number was either used for what, over the years, had become a subsidiary working or had completely disappeared and so he or she arranged for the routes to be renumbered in October to the confusion of the travelling public. There were two cases of this happening - the 53A, the suffix of which indicated it ran via Blackheath rather than Woolwich Road, was renumbered 53 and, as illustrated here, the Sunday 27 to Hounslow and the daily 27A to Teddington swopped numbers. Chalk Farm had a Sunday allocation on the Teddington route and whilst someone has painted out the A on the badly wound destination blind they have omitted the canopy blind which must have been very helpful to westbound passengers in Richmond. SRT112 is the bewildered bus.

(D.A. Ruddom collection)

These interior views of LTC12 taken on the 1st August show that, incredibly, the original seating as fitted to these 1937/38 Weymann built coaches is still in place. Interesting features include the courier's seat, nicely dropped down for the intending occupant and which folded back into the rear front bulkhead. Luggage racks are in place along practically the length of the coach and window winders are provided in the top of the window frames. Each pair of seats was staggered and covered in cloth except for the head rest area and the hard wearing edges which were finished in leather. All of this class of 24 vehicles had been withdrawn from service by the end of the year. (J.C. Gillham)

RT52, delivered new to London Transport in 1940, had been one of a small number to be used to familiarise drivers for the forthcoming deliveries of the post-war 3RT3 way back in 1947. It spent some time at Croydon and Old Kent Road garages in 1948 but now it has returned to its usual routes from Putney Bridge garage, having received an overhaul in the intervening period. Now displaying some dents and even a suspicion of body sag, it waits at Putney Bridge Station on route 93.

With the crossroads at South Wimbledon Station in the background, D71 and RT139 pick up their respective passengers for the journey either to St. Helier Avenue or Epsom Station. Long gone are the days when so many passengers boarded buses at this stop that it was thought necessary to segregate them into orderly queues, the nearer of the two for Morden Station, North Cheam and Epsom and the further one for St. Helier on Mondays to Fridays only. (Lens of Sutton)

St. Mary's Square, Hitchin is the location of this 5th April view showing Green Line T621 with blinds set for the 303B route over to Broomin Green at Stevenage. Is the driver wondering why the bus should be showing such a blind or is he merely checking that it is the correct one? (A.B. Cross)

The date is Saturday the 5th April and TF19 works from Hertford garage on route 390. Seen here at the White Lion, Stevenage, the route's northern terminus, the bus carries a good load of ladies returning from what was then the shopping centre for the area. The well dressed driver carries a ticket box, which must mean he is employed on a route using Cs, although why he should be waiting at this point is not clear. He wears a fine good fitting winter overcoat with white band at the bottom of his right arm for extra clarity when giving hand signals. In the background is one of the elegant bus shelters built in the later 1930s and common in the outlying country area during the period. The air of a country market town, still just discernible in Stevenage Old Town today, pervades the picture and it will be a few years yet before the shoppers transfer their affections to the multiple stores of the New Town centre. (A.B. Cross)

Park Street, Luton, on the 28th June with TF49 waiting to take its next turn on route 364 through the villages to Hitchin. About to pass it is Luton Corporation number 85, a utility Bristol K6A, with black painted radiator shell and Park Royal 56 seat body bound for Stopsley. The buildings in the background were demolished many years ago to make way for the present day Luton College of Higher Education. (A.B. Cross)

On the 8th January brand new red liveried RTL1258 operates on Country Area route 405 while on short-term loan to Reigate garage. It moved to Barking garage in the Central area a few days after this picture was taken in company with several of its Leyland contemporaries which had also been assisting in various parts of the "green" area. The route number under the canopy was permanently illuminated, a practice later discontinued and is not necessarily a sign of deteriorating light conditions. (A.B. Cross)

The highest numbered of the Central Area single deck LT class acquired from the LGOC on 1st July 1933 was LT1201. It is seen here in Kingsley Road beside the old Hounslow garage while starting another run on route 237 to Chertsey.
(J.C. Gillham)

An interesting scene at Morden Underground Station on the 22nd November. The four D class buses now face in the opposite direction to that seen in photographs which have appeared in earlier years in this series of books. From left to right are Duple lowbridge bodied D131, Park Royal bodied D189, Duple highbridge bodied D89 and to the far right Brush bodied D102. The products from the three body builders used for the D class are therefore shown in this very representative selection. (J.C. Gillham)

Another view showing the unusual stand arrangement that occurred during 1952 at Kingston Bus Station. Over seventeen years separate the date of the entry into service of T24 and T734. T24 carries the very detailed slip board giving three different minimum fares applicable to routes 215, 218 and 219 to protect accommodation for longer distance travellers boarding in Kingston. (D.W.K. Jones)

A scattering of snow alongside Enfield garage on the 15th March provides a cold resting place for G146. Someone has thoughtfully provided a blanket to prevent the radiator freezing up. A Park Royal bodied example delivered in July 1945 to the Board, it commenced service in a livery of brown and yellow ochre, with pinkish-brown roof and moquette seating. It gained a repaint into normal London Transport fleet livery in August 1948 and an overhaul in June 1951 and now no trace of its former outrageous colours remain. (J.C. Gillham)

The 6th stage of the tram replacement programme took place on the 5th/6th January and three members of the RT class, having recently been put into service from Rye Lane garage await their departures from Grove Park Station on their new routes. From left to right are RT2754 on route 149 to Cannon St. Stn., formerly tram 52; RT2733 ready for route 179 to Farringdon St., previously tram 74 and RT3391, the driver of which is searching through the blind for Victoria on route 69, formerly tram 54. (C.F. Klapper. Omnibus Society)

Standing on the forecourt of Dorking garage on the 25th May, RT3125 of Dorking works the 429/439 group of routes as is evident from the confused blind displays. These routes formed a circle from Dorking to Newdigate with 439 starting at Newdigate and completing three quarters of the circle before striking off at a tangent at Gadbrook Cross Roads for Redhill. The duty shown probably ran clockwise to Newdigate as a 429 and then became a 439 completing the circle back to Dorking and continuing again via Brockham but then turning off through Leigh to Redhill. (J.F. Bearman)

On loan from the Country Area, Green Line liveried T566 disgorges its load of passengers in Cromwell Road, Kingston. The driver has reset the blind for the next journey on route 213 through to Belmont Station.

Seen here with the southern gateway to the Blackwall Tunnel in the background, STL1884 stands outside a typical tobacconist's shop front. Operating on route 108A to Eltham, Southend Crescent, which was a deviant of route 108, this type of STL was specially built to operate through the Blackwall and Rotherhithe Tunnels. They were always classified 4/9STL13 with the exception of odd man out STL834 which was a 1/9STL13 receiving the body originally carried by STL1854 after it was rebuilt in 1944. STL2437 the other 'tunnel bus' carrying a fleet number outside the 1800 series, was, in fact, a normal 4/9 STL13. (C. Carter)

The rows of gleaming new RT family buses at Edgware garage, waiting entry into service on the various tram replacement schemes, have now given way to the unwanted London buses. The Guys were always unpopular with drivers, both in terms of comfort and performance and so they were the first major class of "utilities" to go. In this view from left to right, G195, 165, 173, 107 and 210 all wait their eventual fate, which is well documented in the PSV Circle publication 2LT3 which deals with the wartime B, D and G classes. (Lens of Sutton)

Sister vehicles RT2936 and 2937 displaying their pristine newness appear to have been selected by Willesden garage to undertake some type of private hire duty. They were delivered to Willesden in July and obviously have not yet seen a lot of employment. (Roy Marshall)

The South Suburban Co-Operative Society Limited premises in the background remind one of the days when this smaller type of retail premises was commonplace. Nowadays they have been overtaken by the superstores and newly overhauled RT850 is also but a memory. Here the bus plies on route 130, which, on 22nd October, had been extended north to Streatham Common via Galpins Road, Rowan Road and Streatham Vale to provide a service to this area from Croydon for the first time. (Roy Marshall)

TF9 was withdrawn in May of this year, being disposed of to W. North Ltd. some months later, thereby ending a little piece of history. Built for private hire and touring work back in 1939 the coach was the only survivor of a small batch of 12. The other 11 members all lost their lives in the disastrous bombing of the Bull Yard, Peckham on 23rd October 1940. This batch of coaches, together with LTC1-24 comprised the standard pre-war private hire luxury coach fleet and were eventually replaced by RF1-25, and the RFW class in 1951. Standing outside the compound next to Gillingham Street garage, which in later years was to earn the grandiose title of Wilton Road Coach Station, the coach still looks to be in good shape amongst the wind blown litter with RT4080 laying over on a short working of route 2. (C. Carter)

When the new Garston garage opened on 18th June, the poky premises at Leavesden Road were closed. To get an idea of how poky, have a look at the photograph on page 92 of the 1950 book in this series. It meant that no longer was the WT code to be seen in Watford. Here, on a very wet day before that closure Q78 bears the WT code as it stops opposite Watford Junction Station while working route 318 to Abbots Langley. It is probably a Saturday since it is followed by a Central Area SRT on loan for the day and working out to Luton on route 321. Q78 was to have an exotic end to its career, being exported to Libya in 1954 where it was operated at least until October 1956 by "Unione Tripolina Autotransporti". (C. Carter)

A further interesting view of the vehicles stored inside Reigate garage is revealed in this panoramic view of a line up of CR class buses. From left to right are CRs26 and 7 with all engine compartment panelling removed allowing the opportunity to see the engine arrangement. Then CRs22 and 29 appear to be in "as withdrawn" condition although the former has lost its bottom panel and foglight whilst the line is completed by the rear view of CR30 complete with all panelling albeit somewhat dented. (John Gascoine collection)

A small number of the delightful CR class were still in use in 1952 and CR13 is seen here in East Grinstead on the 24th May. Route 494 operated between East Grinstead and Oxted through roads and with loadings which made the use of the rear engined Leyland REC, 20 seat buses appropriate. (D.W.K. Jones)

RT117 heads a line of vehicles waiting to take horse racing enthusiasts to the Epsom Race Course meeting in June while a speeding car passes in the opposite direction. The age of the vehicles used on this service has considerably improved as a glance at pictures of buses on this service in earlier volumes will show. One wonders what the significance was of the chalked "X" on the RT's front mudguard. (D.W.K. Jones)

As described in the 1951 book, the local Eastern National routes in Grays and Tilbury were acquired by London Transport on 30th September 1951 and from then until 2nd January 1952 they continued to be operated separately using a mixture of former E.N.O.C. vehicles and STLs. Immediately prior to the rationalisation of these routes additional RT class vehicles were allocated to Grays ready for the new scheme which became operative on the 2nd January. Here on the previous day RT4119 operates route 57 which disappeared next day being replaced by route 357 covering the same roads from Nutberry Corner to Tilbury Docks. Passing in the opposite direction is an Austin 10 "Litchfield" saloon, first introduced in 1934. (A.B. Cross)

Red liveried RTL791 emerges from the forecourt of St. Albans garage on the 28th June on the long haul to Uxbridge L.T. Station of route 351. RTL loans to the Country Area at weekends were an occasional phenomenon and Garston garage, which had only been open a fortnight when this picture was taken, was often supplied such vehicles by Central Area garages in north-west London. (A.B. Cross)

Kew Green has always been liked by the photographer of the London bus as there was little or no interference from other road users and at certain times the sun is just in the right position. This fine view in July sunshine of recently overhauled RT490 operating from Middle Row garage confirms this. The picture exuberates the atmosphere of days long gone. The final destination blind has yet to be changed for its return journey back across the River Thames. The timetable panel fixed to the lamp post is interesting since there does not appear to be any associated bus stop flag and it is unlikely passengers would be permitted to board at this stand on the off-side of the road. (J.H. Aston)

Rye Lane garage in Bellenden Road, Peckham, had opened in January and gained further work in April when the two remaining Kingsway Subway tram services were replaced. Here RT2844 heads for Forest Hill Station in typical south London surroundings on route 172, which replaced the 35 tram. Five and a half years later the former Subway routes 171 and 172 were to swop their southern terminals but for the moment the tramway tradition remained. (W.J. Haynes)

Certain locations were greatly favoured by photographers as is evident when one looks through this series of books. The terminal stand by the Wraysbury River near the former Great Western Railway station at Staines was one of these places and here on 9th February the ultimate SRT, 160, waits to return to Kew Gardens Station on route 90. Built on the converted 4/9STL chassis of STL2438, this bus was delivered new to Harrow Weald, transferred to Twickenham for the 90 and 90B four months later and ended its days at Cricklewood before the body was to gain a new identity as green RT4544. (A.B. Cross)

Almost as if posed for official photographs, RT1831, a 3RT8 in the top picture offers a good comparison with RT246, a 3RT3 below. Both vehicles have Park Royal built bodies and the latter bus has received full blinds on overhaul. RT1831 was one of the last batch to be delivered with the restricted display and as yet has not been converted. Both views were taken on the same day at Crystal Palace and illustrate the shared allocation between Bromley and Catford garages on this route. (J.H. Aston)

In the last year of service with London Transport, STL2220 is seen at Rayners Lane. This bus was yet a further example to be fitted with one of the new lowbridge variety of bodies during the war. These bodies were originally intended for a similar number of new "unfrozen" AEC Regent chassis. Since the new chassis were delivered more quickly they received an assortment of bodies including some of the new STL17 variety. The intended new lowbridge bodies constructed at Chiswick Works were then mounted on newly overhauled chassis. These buses, familiar denizens of the 230 route, were replaced by RLHs before the year was out but between 1953 and 1955 you could still have made a journey on this STL as it was then operated by Bolton-by-Bowland Motor Services Ltd. of Clitheroe. (Geoff Morant)

During 1952, as mentioned in the introduction, three buses representing the two chassis and two main bodybuilders of RT family vehicles were used on what has probably become the most memorable tour to use London Transpsort vehicles, that to North America. Upon their return in August a welcoming ceremony was held on Horse Guards Parade and here on the 20th are, from left to right, RT2775, RTL1307 and RT2776, together with the Leyland Comet MTE910 and Fordson XWT46 support vehicles which accompanied them. The tour had been the brain child of the British Travel and Holidays Association to support tourism and the buses carried suitable advertising for Cunard, BOAC and Jaguar Cars as well as smaller advertising for other national institutions. (D.W.K. Jones)

Although the date is 29th March, snow and slush make travelling just that little bit more tedious to the large crowds of would-be passengers at Morden Station. Green liveried STL2229, a lowbridge example, has been loaned to Merton garage from Godstone for use on route 127 which required such buses. Also identifiable in the picture is STL1630 working from Streatham garage on route 118 while D class buses abound together with a solitary RT. (A.B. Cross)

TF class coaches were still being used on 10th April from Epping, as evidenced in this picture, although a further batch of new RF coaches were then being delivered to the garage. The coach stop in Aldgate bus station carries clear indication that the 720 is the only route to use this particular stop, which stands by the rudimentary canteen. (J.C. Gillham)

The bus stop by Enfield garage provides the setting for G144, a Park Royal bodied 1/3G8 variant on the 30th January. Although 435 utility Guys were delivered only a relatively small proportion received the colour scheme of post-war years which had a single cream band in between decks. The Aberdare Cafe building is topped with a most unusual architectural feature like a miniature observatory. Your guess is as good as mine as to its purpose. (A.B. Cross)

Just days after this rear view of red STL1873 was taken on the 22nd March, the bus moved over to Grays garage as a trainer. Here it is seen on the Epping garage forecourt looking out to the main A11 road. The bus will turn left and follow this road through Epping Town and on to Bishops Stortford, one of the most northerly towns of the London Transport area. (A.B. Cross)

TF70 clearly shows the only alteration necessary when it was demoted to bus work from Green Line duties with its new fleet name. Epping, Dorking, Grays, Luton and St. Albans were the only garages operating this class of 2TF2 on Green Line duties prior to the delivery of the new RF class. Here, on the 1st June, the vehicle stands opposite St. Albans garage on its journey south to Radlett. (A.B. Cross)

Ponders End, at the junction of Hertford Road and Southbury Road, on the 30th January. Under the trolleybus wiring for the Waltham Cross routes G313 turns sharply to make its way through Enfield and Oakwood on a short working to New Barnet. This very angular product from the body builder Massey, who had supplied 49 similar vehicles to London Transport, would not be seen on the streets of the capital for much longer as it was withdrawn from service the following month. Edinburgh Corporation, to whom it was despatched in April, rebuilt the chassis, had a new Duple Midland (Nudd) double deck body mounted and re-registered the vehicle making it completely unrecognisable. (A.B. Cross)

When Alperton garage received RTs for the 83 route in July there was a shortage of new blinds and so several brand new vehicles entered service with the masked display of earlier years. RT2915 was one such vehicle and it stands at Alperton Station on 21st August en route from Golders Green to Ealing while the driver has a quiet doze on the steering wheel. (A.B. Cross)

T728, from the batch of fifty 14T12 class delivered in 1946 and bodied by Weymann, stands outside the Staines Baptist Church before making a return journey to Kingston. Although the opening of the new Norbiton garage in May affected many allocations in the Kingston area, the majority of the 216 route operations remained with Kingston garage. (Omnibus Society. J.F. Higham)

Harrow Weald received four STL class vehicles for new Monday to Saturday route 209, Harrow Weald Garage to South Harrow Station via Pinner and Rayners Lane which started on 14th May. Here, on the 31st of that month, former Edgware garage STL715 is at South Harrow. (A.B. Cross)

Oh, to buy a bottle of "Rich Ruby Wine" for 6/- (now 30p) but in 1952 you could do just that. The second batch of NCME bodied Guys lacked the rather heavy front window ventilators of their predecessors. While doubtless not improving the air quality of the upper deck, the appearance of the vehicles was greatly enhanced. Here G233 grinds up Barnet Hill on the 14th January en route to the Arkley Hotel. (A.B. Cross)

On the stand at Orpington Station, RTL1025 waits to return to Sidcup on route 229. In October this route was to be further extended to Bexleyheath but on 18th May, when this picture was taken, Wren Road was still the north-eastern extremity of the route. The bus is a Park Royal bodied example which has yet to receive full blinds. (J.H. Aston)

RTL566 in Enfield Town shows the unmistakeable visible difference between the Metro Cammell bodied product and other builder's examples by its thinner cream band and prominent beading between the decks. Following the RTL on 10th May is STD38, another Enfield garage vehicle, transferred there early in 1952, having been ousted from its long term home at Hendon by newer vehicles. (A.B. Cross)

Another member of the SRT class always allocated to Chalk Farm garage was SRT103, seen here at the South End Green, Hampstead Heath terminus of Route 24. Only 48 of this class of 160 vehicles were ever given overhauls before being withdrawn from service and the bodies remounted on to new RT chassis. Ex 15STL, STL2598 provided the chassis and mechanical running units for this SRT and the body was later used to produce RT4509, one of the examples allocated to Green Line work from Grays. (J.C. Gillham)

Battered and forlorn looking G427 resides at Edgware garage in company with Q213 and further double deckers. Its Weymann body must have been considered as beyond repair since early in 1953 the vehicle was noted in Aberdeen in use as a lorry. (John Gascoine collection)

RT3455, RTL917 and two further unidentifiable RTs are a long way from the streets of London. They are seen here on Southsea Common on private hire duties on the 15th June. Note the shallower cream band carried between decks by the RTL, a giveaway to the fact that it carries one of the all metal bodies by Metro-Cammell, a company who only bodied 450 of the RT family vehicles, all on Leyland chassis. (J.F. Bearman)

The three buses, having returned from their glorious tour of the North American continent, were put on show at the Earls Court Exhibition Hall forecourt in West Brompton at the time of the 1952 Commercial Motor Show. On the 29th September, nearest the camera, flag bedecked RT2775 stands with RTL1307 and RT2776 distinguishable with its additional ventilator grills in the roof. The nose of the Fordson 10cwt. van which accompanied the three buses on their tour can just be seen farthest away in the line up: while a Humber 'Pullman' stands to the left of the line up of tour vehicles.
(J.F. Bearman)

Recently overhauled RT988 has been returned to Northfleet garage who first received it when new in 1948. Route 480 at the time proceeded east of Gravesend to Denton but here the bus is to work short to the Clock Tower in the centre of the town. (Lens of Sutton)

The date is the 1st January and ex-red STL1720 enters Grays High Street to terminate on the former ENOC 32A route. Next day the route would still be running between Grays and Nutberry Corner via Southend Road and Lodge Lane but under the LT number 323A. (A.B. Cross)

The drab interior of a Massey bodied Guy, G261, shows clearly the rexine seating on wooden frames fitted to this body builder's products for London. All forward facing seats included grab handles incorporated into the back squabs and the total effect was spartan. While the exterior of most of these vehicles when delivered was an all over ginger brown, the interior effect was brown - and more brown! (J.C. Gillham)

It is the 15th January and Hertford based Q238 is dressed for its usual stint on Green Line route 715. During the year the arrival of the remainder of the Green Line RF coaches spelt the end of the road for these side engined coaches on this route on which they had been familiar operators, apart from the war years, since they were delivered in 1936/37. After a spell in storage Q238, along with twenty three other members of the 6Q6 sub class, had a few months reprieve operating in the Central Area from Muswell Hill garage until they were returned to store in October, never again to see London service. (A.B. Cross)

Route 98A was a new weekday connection in west London introduced on 16th April running between Hounslow and the Red Lion at Pinner where Uxbridge's RT2133 is seen on the last day of May in company with Hendon's STD59 on the 183 route. (A.B. Cross)

This further view from the Sabena Airlines' archives taken at Melsbroek Airport of ex LT Guys gives an idea of the basic terminal facilities available in 1952. The airport has now of course grown out of all recognition, on similar lines to that of London's air terminals. The helicopter, still relatively uncommon in 1952, has attracted the attention of the passengers. (Sabena Belgian World Airlines)

Another view of the temporary terminus north of Hammersmith Bridge as announced by the slip boards of these two buses on route 73. RTL309 leads the line-up as they wait to return to Stoke Newington. Air France seems to be conducting a strong advertising campaign for travel to destinations far from its home country. (A.B. Cross)

TF51 seen in Park Street, Luton, was together with TF55, seen earlier in this book, two of Luton garaged long-stay coaches demoted to bus work upon the delivery of RF166 - 173 in January of this year. The blind is one of those peculiar to Luton which never correctly fitted the blind boxes giving this rather untidy display. The Birch Brothers vehicle on the other side of the road is KXU670, which was the first Leyland CP01 with Windover coachwork delivered to that operator in 1949. (A.B. Cross)

APPENDIX I

London Transport Central and Country Area Bus Garages

A	Sutton	HW	Southall
AB	Twickenham	J	Holloway
AC	Willesden	K	Kingston
AD	Palmers Green	L	Loughton
AE	Hendon	LH*	Leatherhead
AF	Chelverton Road, Putney	LS*	Luton
AH	Nunhead	M	Mortlake
AK	Streatham	MA*	Amersham
AL	Merton	MH	Muswell Hill
AM	Plumstead	N	Norwood
AP	Seven Kings	NF*	Northfleet
AR	Tottenham	ON	Alperton
AV	Hounslow	P	Old Kent Road
B	Battersea	PB	Potters Bar
BK	Barking	PM	Peckham
BN	Brixton	Q	Camberwell
C	Athol Street, Poplar	R	Riverside
CA	Clapham	RD	Hornchurch
CF	Chalk Farm	RE*	Romford, London Road
CL	Clay Hall	RG*	Reigate
CM*	Chelsham	S	Shepherds Bush
CS	Chiswick (non-operational)	SA*	St Albans
CY*	Crawley	SJ*	Swanley Junction
D	Dalston	SP	Sidcup
DG*	Dunton Green	ST*	Staines
DS*	Dorking	T	Leyton
DT*	Dartford	TB	Bromley
E	Enfield	TC	Croydon
ED	Elmers End	TG*	Tring
EG*	East Grinstead	TH	Thornton Heath
EP*	Epping	TL	Catford
EW	Edgware	TW*	Tunbridge Wells
F	Putney Bridge	U	Upton Park
G	Forest Gate	UX	Uxbridge
GA*	Argent Street, Grays	V	Turnham Green
GD*	Godstone	W	Cricklewood
GF*	Guildford	WA*	Watford, High Street
GM	Gillingham Street, Victoria	WD	Wandsworth
GY*	Grays	WG	West Green
H	Hackney	WL	Walworth
HD	Harrow Weald	WR*	Windsor
HE*	High Wycombe	WT*	Watford, Leavesden Road
HF*	Hatfield	WY*	Addlestone
HG*	Hertford	X	Middle Row
HH*	Two Waters, Hemel Hempstead	-	Aldenham (non-operational)
HN*	Hitchin		

*indicates a Country Area garage.

The above list is of all operational garages plus the two main non-operational sites for bus maintenance available on 1st January 1952.

During the year two garages were closed, both in the Country Area:

GA after operations on 1st January when the Grays routes were integrated and all operations transferred to GY.
WT after operations on 17th June when the new Garston (GR) garage was opened.

Six garages were opened during the year:

AW Abbey Wood on 6th July being converted from a tram depot. Initially only the buses for route 177 and 182 (Suns) worked from AW, those for the 186 and 161 (Suns) being outstationed at AM until building works were completed.
GR Garston on 18th June. The only new Country Area garage which allowed the closure of WT and a redistribution of the work of WA.
NB Norbiton on 14th May absorbing much of the work of the overcrowded Kingston (K) garage.
NX New Cross which ceased operation as a tram depot on the night of 5th/6th July. Initially the replacing buses operated out of PM, Q and RL garages although NX plates were carried and NX crews operated the vehicles. Operations were completely returned to NX by 12th November.
RL Rye Lane on 6th January, being built on the site formerly used by the tram track maintenance department in Bellenden Road. Oddly, despite its name it had no physical connection with Rye Lane.
SW Stockwell on 2nd April. For its first four days this vast new garage only operated 11 buses on route 178 until the tram conversion on 6th April when it gained the new 171 route.

This is one of the thirty C class vehicles to be exported to Belgium immediately after World War II had ended. Although the Belgian registration 272242 is easily read very little information on these vehicles in their new surroundings is documented and any information about them would be keenly welcomed. (A.B. Cross)

APPENDIX II

Thanks to correspondence from interested enthusiasts the following information is provided to up-date captions in previously published books in this series.

1948 BOOK

Page 31   B1 is standing outside the Lido Cinema in Northfield Avenue.

1950 BOOK

Page 42   TD80 stands alongside the Fyffe's banana warehouse in Wood Street, Kingston.

Page 63   ST136 is at the long standing terminus for route 127 in Milner Road opposite South Wimbledon Underground Station.

This picture of TF1, taken on the 17th September 1950 when the coach was operated by Castle Coaches of Lewisham, arrived just too late to be included in the 1950 book. It is included here, not simply because it was the only 1TF1 built, but also for the pleasing, well proportioned, albeit altered lines of its LPTB built bodywork. The driver's cab area was rebuilt from the original, almost glass house like, appearance in June 1940 bringing it more in line with the production batch of Green Line coaches, although there were still minor exterior differences. The most notable being the sloping down of the foremost windows to the saloon and the level finish gained to the bottom of all the front windows. The step up in the window line towards the rear of the vehicle, a carry over from the 9T9 and 10T10 classes was not continued on the production batch. The Leyland Motors badge beneath the windscreen was a much later addition. Photographed here at a convenient lay-over stop at Nutley between Forest Row and Uckfield, one assumes the L sticker refers to some private hire activity rather than indicating a small learner! (J.C. Gillham)

1951 BOOK

Page 60   T22 is outside the YMCA building in Eden Street, Kingston.

Page 88   LT1168 is at the "Black Horse", East Sheen and not Barnes Common as captioned.

Page 133   STL1731 is at Raynes Park just prior to turning on to the stand in Kingston Road.